Your Towns and Cities in the

The Black Country
in the Great War

Your Towns and Cities in the Great War

The Black Country in the Great War

Michael Pearson

Pen & Sword
MILITARY

First published in Great Britain in 2014 by
PEN & SWORD MILITARY
an imprint of
Pen and Sword Books Ltd
47 Church Street
Barnsley
South Yorkshire S70 2AS

ISBN 978 1 78337 608 7

Printed and bound in England
by CPI Group (UK) Ltd, Croydon, CR0 4YY

Typeset in Times New Roman by Chic Graphics

Pen & Sword Books Ltd incorporates the imprints of
Pen & Sword Archaeology, Atlas, Aviation, Battleground, Discovery,
Family History, History, Maritime, Military, Naval, Politics, Railways,
Select, Social History, Transport, True Crime, Claymore Press,
Frontline Books, Leo Cooper, Praetorian Press, Remember When,
Seaforth Publishing and Wharncliffe.

For a complete list of Pen and Sword titles please contact
Pen and Sword Books Limited
47 Church Street, Barnsley, South Yorkshire, S70 2AS, England
E-mail: enquiries@pen-and-sword.co.uk
Website: www.pen-and-sword.co.uk

Contents

Acknowledgements

Every project I undertake is first of all discussed with my greatest supporter, copy typist and 'sufferer', my wife Lin. She has always been supportive of my work, even though she may hide thoughts such as 'Not again' or 'What this time?' I also want to thank Pen and Sword for allowing me to combine two passions of mine: the Black Country and military history. The latter stems from schooldays with my history teacher, Barry Miles, a Welshman who looked a little like Ernie Wise, and the former is due to my own research into my ancestors, Woodside miners born and bred. I quickly became diverted into more general Black Country local history research and thanks to Stan Hill, I joined the band of enthusiasts on the committee of the Black Country Society.

I also want to thank the staff at the Black Country Living Museum, especially Jo Moody and Helen Taylor, for their assistance and cooperation. We are all looking into the Great War and have been able to feed from each other with regard to research material. My gratitude goes to Dave Kerr from the Birmingham and Midland Society for Genealogy and Heraldry for his sharing of family research; and finally, to Doctor Paul Collins for allowing me to use images from his collection.

Images

Images in this book have been obtained from a number of sources. Those obtained directly have been duly acknowledged but some have been acquired on the open market and, despite attempts at tracing their origin, many remain anonymous. These images are normally credited to the 'collection' of the author. Ownership of a print of a photograph or a copy of a postcard does not confer copyright upon the owner. In such instances copyright rests with the original photographer, the company for whom the image was taken, or the person, organization or company to whom copyright has been assigned. Again, such photographs are usually credited to the 'collection' contributor. If, through no fault of my own, photographs or images have been used without due credit or acknowledgement, my apologies are offered. If anyone believes this to be the case, please let me know and the necessary credit will be added at the earliest opportunity.

CHAPTER 1

Introduction

The Black Country border

When researching and writing, as my self-imposed border for material I use the four boroughs that form the Black Country part of the wider West Midlands: Dudley, Sandwell, Walsall and Wolverhampton. Occasionally I stray outside these boundaries, especially if the information is of sufficient interest and relevance to the subject. This may not be everyone's idea or view of the Black Country but it does make research more straightforward.

The Black Country is that area of what is now the West Midlands that lies to the west of Birmingham. At the time of the First World War it was divided between Staffordshire and Worcestershire. Major towns include Walsall, Wolverhampton, West Bromwich and Dudley, the latter being the 'unofficial' (but disputed) capital of the region.

The Black Country has no specific geographic boundary; its traditional area is that land that sits above the 30-foot-thick South Staffordshire coal seam. This loosely-defined boundary has led to many debates and disputes about who is and who isn't in the Black Country, which means there are as many interpretations as there are people who have an opinion on the subject. I choose to use the four boundaries containing sections of that earlier definition: Dudley, Wolverhampton, Walsall and Sandwell. This may be something of a 'cop-out' but it does make my research much easier as I can use material from the four archives, one for each metropolitan borough.

Background to the Black Country

At the turn of the twentieth century the Black Country was a major industrial area and had been a large contributor to the development of the British Empire throughout the reign of Queen Victoria. Industrialization was at a peak and this would be a crucial factor during the war in terms of the manufacture of munitions and weapons, including the introduction of the tank to combat. As the war progressed, the Black Country looked like one huge munitions works, producing much of the country's ammunition as well as tanks and other essential equipment. This war changed the shape of the Black Country forever; not only physically because of the building work needed to service the munitions industry but also socially.

The greatest social changes involved women: as more and more men went into the armed services, demand for essential workers created opportunities – and threats – for women. Prior to the war, women had largely been 'stay-at-home' housewives and mothers to large families with only a small proportion of them going out to work. During the war women became clerks, factory workers, tram drivers, leather workers and carried out a whole range of other jobs. Only four years before the war began, women chainmakers from Cradley Heath fought a bitter strike to break themselves out of the 'slavery' imposed on them by unscrupulous employers who paid them as little as 1d an hour. This strike would lead to the first nationally-agreed minimum wage and began the end of the so-called 'sweated' trades.

By the end of the war women over the age of 30 were granted the right to vote and were also allowed to stand for Parliament. Women became more than housewives and mothers: they worked in factories, on trams, in offices; in fact in any workplace where they were needed to replace the men who had gone to war. Some men in the Black Country were exempted from being called up. Mining and heavy industry was essential war work and the workforce had to be maintained and protected. However, this would change in the latter years of the war, as needs dictated.

Weapons and munitions have become much more sophisticated over the centuries and in the early twentieth century their production took a great proportion of the output of our industries. It was these joint demands that inevitably led to great change in the Black Country during and after more than four years of war. From this large population centre many men volunteered or were called up to fight; that process starting right from the commencement of conflict. This denuded many employers of valuable workers but their jobs still had to be done and this led to the employment of women in traditionally male occupations.

Companies such as George Salter & Co., a well-known firm based in West Bromwich, adapted their business for the war. They had been on the Admiralty and War Office list of suppliers for some years prior to the war and immediately became 'government controlled' in 1914, meaning that they could no longer take private orders without permission.

The prelude to war

War in 1914 came as no surprise to many. The seeds were sown many years previously when in 1900 Archduke Franz Ferdinand married Countess Sophie Chotek, a Czech aristocrat from the then kingdom of Bohemia. He was heir to the monarch of the Habsburgs; Sophie was not Imperial Habsburg material and could never become Her Imperial Highness. She did not belong to one of the reigning or former reigning European dynasties. The only recognition the archduke could give to his wife was when he acted in his military capacity. This would lead to the fateful event in 1914 in Sarajevo.

Bosnia and Herzegovina was annexed by Austro-Hungary in 1908 and there was much resentment of the Habsburgs. The archduke announced that he would be inspecting the army, accompanied by Sophie (now Duchess), in an open carriage at Sarajevo on 28 June. This was their wedding anniversary and the inspection was an anniversary present for his beloved. There were real risks involved in this visit as the date was also the anniversary of the Battle of Kosovo Polje in 1389 which went down in Serbian myth and poetry as a cataclysmic defeat for Serbia, leading to the Turks sweeping through and conquering the country.

There were no fewer than six assassins in the crowd when the royal party drove through Sarajevo. Five failed to act and the sixth threw a bomb, which bounced off Franz Ferdinand's car. Then a wrong turn took the car into Franz Josef Street where Gavrilo Princip spotted the archduke's vehicle stationary in front of him. Princip jumped on to the running board and fired twice into the car, hitting both the archduke and Sophie. They died a slow, agonizing death and exactly one month later Austro-Hungary declared war on Serbia. The Great War began soon after.

Five great European powers faced off against each other. Germany and Britain were generally on friendly terms. France, Britain's old enemy, was also becoming friendlier towards Germany but there was apprehension regarding the lumbering giant that was Russia. Now that Austro-Hungary had decided to act against Serbia, alliances would be tested. Germany backed Austro-Hungary and Russia supported Serbia. It took time for events to unfold but slowly and inexorably Europe moved towards war.

'The die is cast', was the chilling report as Germany declared war on Russia. On the following day German forces marched into Luxembourg and crossed the French frontier in Lorraine without declaring war. It was reported that Germany and Austro-Hungary acted because of what had happened in Sarajevo, though complicity by the Serbian government had not been proved. Russia sprang to the defence of Serbia, began to mobilize and within twelve hours Germany declared war on Russia. Germany summoned France, the next domino in the line and an ally of Russia, to remain neutral and it was now the turn of France to mobilize.

By the beginning of August millions of men were mobilized ready for war: Europe was a tinderbox that now had its spark. The Germans marched through Belgium, bringing about Britain's entry into the war on 4 August. Britain declared war on Germany and the Kaiser quickly retaliated by declaring war on Britain in front of a large crowd in Berlin.

Our story begins here, with the British Expeditionary Force (BEF) being mobilized. By 22 August it had reached Mons in Belgium but what was life like back at home? This is the reason for this book. It is not an examination of the events during the war, which have already been ably covered by many writers and no doubt many more such titles will be released during 2014. No, I am interested only in what happened in the Black Country, an area critical to British success in the war.

This was billed as 'the war to end all wars'. It brought about changes to the roles and lives of women, society, religion and politics; subjects that will be explored throughout the book. The nature of how wars were fought changed: the sheer numbers involved, the inevitable development of new weapons such as tanks and aircraft, and the tactics used to wage war.

CHAPTER 2

1914:
Eager for a Fight

Timeline of events

- 4 August: War declared by Britain, triggered by the German invasion of Belgium
- 7 August: First units of BEF land in France
- 8 August: Defence of the Realm Act passed
- 20 August: Brussels occupied by German forces
- 24 August: Battle of Mons begins
- 5 September: End of retreat from Mons
- 1 October: First Battle of Arras begins
- 10 October: Antwerp capitulates to Germans
- 19 October: Battle of Ypres begins
- 5 November: Britain and France declare war on Turkey
- 22 November: Battle of Ypres ends
- 21 December: First German air-raid on England (Dover)
- 24 December: First bomb lands on Dover town in second raid

This chapter explores the build-up to war and the recruitment of men to the BEF. There were emotional and exciting scenes as families and crowds said goodbye to their men, with services and parades taking place. Local politicians played a large part in the Black Country, especially in the early months when recruitment was crucial. Industry had to gear up for war but the scale of this only became apparent over time. There were massive changes in legislation and working practices, all of which affected the region. Many believed that the conflict would soon be concluded and it is doubtful that anyone foresaw the bitter and bloody war that was to follow.

A call to arms

'The Day Has Come!' declared the newspapers. The British government had not rushed into war in a panic but Germany's actions left them no option other than to declare war. Britain entered into war with clean hand and confident heart. Entry was 'secured' when Germany invaded neutral Belgium, which the British had pledged to protect.

Britain did not have a large enough standing army to fight the imminent conflict. Initially there was reliance on reservists and the Territorials. On 1 August 1914 there was a call to arms for the Territorials locally and in Stourbridge they reported for duty amid great excitement: 'the greatest and unprecedented excitement', stated the oldest resident that could be found in the town. The local Territorials were recalled from their camp at Minehead on Monday, 3 August which presaged the serious state of the situation on the continent. From the early hours of Wednesday the streets began to fill with men, women and children. Thousands congregated at the Drill Hall at 9am; kit inspection followed, with orders to fall in at 2pm. Men walked about

Belgians escape from the Germans.

Worcestershire Reserve Battalion, civic farewell: Dudley, October 1914.

with relatives and friends, some in tears, even though they were only being sent on home duty. At 2pm around Market Street and Hall Street crowds watched the preparations for departure. The National Reserve also mustered under command of Sergeant Major Ward. The company moved off along Bell Street and Market Street towards Stourbridge Junction Railway Station.

A spirit of sober, grim patriotism was recorded: hundreds followed the company, singing *Rule Britannia*, *Three Cheers for the Red, White and Blue* and *Farewell My Own True Love*. Photographers were busy along the route. Captain Grosvenor organized an official photograph for the *County Express* newspaper. At the railway station Police Sergeant Thomas and his constables handled the crowd admirably; the men were on the train by 3pm, headed for Kidderminster. Hundreds of women and children in nearby fields waved and shouted farewells. This was a memorable departure, the first of many but probably the most poignant.

Elsewhere similar scenes were repeated. At Brierley Hill 'E' Company of the Territorials set off with the shrill blasts of a bugle. Two announcements were issued by authority of the king: the first ordered mobilization of the army reservists and another embodied the men of the Territorials. These orders were expected; indeed, the men had returned from camp at St Asaph and were told they must hold themselves in readiness. Men proceeded towards their HQ at the new Drill Hall in Pearson Street, fully equipped and ready to march. They were met by Sergeant Instructor Smith and Colour Sergeant Bird; the latter was one of many Brierley Hill volunteers who had fought in the South African War. A large crowd assembled at Five Ways and another at Pearson Street, men mingling with family and friends; they drew kit from the stores including blankets, socks and trenching tools. By 1am over 100 men had assembled, everyone was in the best of spirits, patriotic songs were sung and the bugler played. By 9am 117 of 121 men had paraded with only four men absent.

Recruitment proceeded in a similar vein during the next few days with reservists continuing to be called up. Five local police officers were called up from the Stourbridge division to rejoin their regiments. The Worcestershire Police Force cancelled all police leave owing to the crisis and all members of the Halesowen force on leave were recalled. The weekly rest day for police officers was abandoned and all holiday leave withdrawn. One officer had just started leave and had cycled to a friend in Hereford, only to find a telegram awaiting him on arrival recalling him for duty. He had another six-hour cycle ride back home.

Many factories and workplaces lost large numbers to the forces, either as reservists or Territorials. Sankey's was one such company: several branches of the business were severely affected but they benefited from substantial orders from the government. Many famous Black Country family names were represented among the officer ranks; they were named in newspaper reports, the most accessible means for people to keep up with events throughout the war. It all seems closer nowadays with reporters in protective equipment reporting from the front. Examples about six weeks into the war included Geoffrey Elwell, gazetted to the Territorials (Terriers) as a lieutenant and Mr Julian Drinkwater of Upper High Street, Wednesbury, who joined the hussars.

In drizzly weather the company moved to Walsall, leaving behind enthusiastic crowds. It was a 10-mile march via Dudley and by midday the Territorials were billeted at the Town Hall in Walsall pending further orders; the men's destination was not yet known to them. The movement of troops was soon not reported in newspapers; any news that might be of interest to the enemy was suppressed. We now know that two companies of soldiers from 7th Battalion Worcester Regiment landed in France on 17 August and that their first engagement was at Mons where there were heavy casualties. Details of heavy allied casualties were not always reported.

These scenes of mobilization were repeated across the Black Country. Everyone was affected: almost all streets in Darlaston and Wednesbury had men who were in the Territorials or were army or navy reservists. Some families had two, three or four members who were mobilized during this early period of the war.

Patriotic fervour hit the Alhambra Theatre in Stourbridge during the first week of the war. Before the rise of the curtain the crossed flags of England and France appeared on the screen with the motto: 'United We Stand.' The vast audience was on their feet at each house; the band played *God Save the King* and *Rule Britannia* with many joining in the singing of the national anthem. When news arrived of the mobilization of reservists and Territorials, a climax was reached when owner Douglas Phelps stepped to the front and read a resumé of the proclamation of His Majesty the King. With stirring words he congratulated reservists and Territorials present on doing their share to keep the Union Jack flying over the Great British Empire. There were scenes of 'indescribable enthusiasm' and about 200 men immediately left the theatre to report themselves.

Defence of the Realm Act 1914

This crucial piece of legislation was quickly passed to give the government the wide-ranging powers needed. These included the ability to requisition buildings or land and to create new criminal offences. There were also sweeping social control measures including censorship, the lighting of bonfires, kite-flying, discussing naval and military activities and strict controls over alcohol.

Censorship applied both in newspapers and to letters sent home from the front; people who breached these regulations with intent to assist the enemy could be sentenced to death. Ten people were executed during the war as a result. Propaganda also played a large part during the conflict: transmitting news of the war, informing the population of the situation, giving advice, tips and updating people on legislation changes. This was principally achieved through local newspapers. Newsboys were seen as heroes of the day, with special editions of newspapers being produced and distributed at all hours of the day and night. Post Offices and telegraph services were reportedly very busy. Post Offices usually closed early on Thursdays but stayed open as late as midnight in the early weeks of the war. Wednesbury Library was crowded with people searching for war news.

The government confiscated the wireless equipment of amateur experts; they were assured it would be returned after the war. News of interest to many Black Country people was the banning of pigeon-racing across the UK within three weeks of the start of the war. This news was broadcast by the National Pigeon Flying Club and the ban was to remove any opportunity for Germans living in England to use races as a cover to release birds to fly to Germany. Compared to today, the government found it easy to suppress communications and ensure that what the public read and heard did not adversely affect morale.

Regulations relating to the sale of alcohol included watering-down alcoholic beverages and restricting the hours that pubs were allowed to open. Eventually times were restricted to noon till 3pm and 6.30 to 9.30pm. This gap in opening hours remained in force until 1988. 'Drink' will be explored in more depth in the chapter titled 'Feeding the Black Country'.

In September the war was still billed as 'exciting' for the troops. One headline read: 'Exciting details of encounters'. A Hill Top resident, Jack Diggett, an able-bodied seaman of the North Sea Fleet was 'still alive and very busy'. His parents described how he had sunk five ships and chased others off: using football analogies they 'won 5–0', not bad as they were 'playing away', 'our forwards shot beautifully, and our defence was sound'. The British lost about 40 dead and 50 wounded, while German losses were over 1,000. They were now preparing for 'the big match of the season'.

In September there was a newspaper report on 'The War and "Parasites"'. Local boards of guardians drew to the attention of local government boards and the War Office details of able-bodied vagrants (aged 18–30 years) in the workhouse. Suggestions were made to utilize their services. Some 'roadsters' had volunteered for active service but the army did not want that 'class' of men. A grim suggestion was that they might be placed in front of better soldiers on the front line. In time, when voluntary recruiting dried up, the enlistment net widened to include classes of men previously ignored.

Not everyone was patriotic, however. John Russell and Co. of Cyclops Ironworks in Walsall summonsed two of their workers, James Allen and James McKenna, for neglect of work. The company had lost about 100 workers to the armed forces and they had agreed to help the wives and children of those men called up. The remaining workers were also paid more money but some went drinking during the firm's time and neglected their work, causing the company to suffer financial loss. McKenna was ordered to pay £3 plus costs. In Allen's case, he had a contract to keep the firm's furnaces supplied with fuel and he employed assistants in this venture. It was said that he failed in his duty and had been seen under the influence of alcohol. He was ordered to pay £4 including costs.

The Under-Secretary for War spoke out on the subject of the seeming reluctance of football professionals, and indeed 'the football crowd' in general, to join the armed forces. The start of war led to the cancellation of all fixtures by amateur rugby clubs. What was wanted was a lead from one or two of the best-known professional players who had not yet responded to their country's call. This would happen eventually; one example was the formation of the 23rd (Service) Battalion Royal Fusiliers (First Sportsman's), which formed in 1914. Many promising footballers joined the armed forces but there were issues about the perception of many young men who had not apparently taken the step to sign up and large crowds of football fans still gathered to watch matches.

Sport was understandably affected by the war. In football, West Bromwich Albion finished fifth in the 1914 season, which concluded just before war broke out. WBA played War Charity and Red Cross matches when they could, fielding those players they could find. One signing for WBA around the war period was Harold Bache, a well-known West Bromwich man and great all-round athlete. Already an amateur international and Cambridge Soccer Blue, he taught English at a university near Amiens in France when approached to join 'The Baggies'. Bache promised to play in the FA Cup against local rivals Aston Villa. He joined the army as a lieutenant and was killed in action with the Lancashire Fusiliers in February 1915, one of many promising sportsmen who perished during the conflict.

By mid-September the impetus of men signing up for the army was waning. A meeting between the mayors of Walsall and Wednesbury resulted in a decision to raise a new battalion for the regular army, following an urgent appeal from the government. They were to be called the Comrades Battalion and a number of these were raised around the country. Men who signed up received a distinctive uniform and those chosen began to drill locally but were 'billeted' at home. Recruiting committees were set up at both Walsall and Wednesbury; their target was to recruit 1,100 men for the battalion.

Some assistance was provided to employers in that there were a number of reserved occupations, which meant that some men could not volunteer. In 1914 there was no legislation to ensure that essential work could continue. For example, miners, police officers, tram workers and Post Office employees joined the armed forces or were recalled as reservists or Territorials. Many shortfalls were filled by women but heavy jobs such as mining and foundry work had to be done by men and restrictions were placed on such workers to prevent them from joining the forces. However, it was not until 1938 that a 'Schedule

In the early years of the war miners were exempt from being called up. This changed as it became a real struggle to find enough men to go to the front in the closing months of the war.

of Reserved Occupations' was created, which included miners and many engineering trades.

Retailers played their part in encouraging normality during the war. F.W. Cook Ltd of Dudley placed adverts like the following, titled 'Patriotism':

> The nation has risen to the crisis magnificently and displayed a united front and grim determination to see the war through. There is a need for patriotism on the part of the purchasing public, so that our home industries and the vast army of workers who furnish the sinews of war may be kept fully employed. To do this, purchase goods as in ordinary times, and thus keep the manufacturers going.

This advert was followed by a message that F.W. Cook would continue buying goods, including new autumn collections of clothing, gowns, etc. Despite the war, fashion was still a hot topic: capes were reported as being fashionable for ladies, often dressed with a flowered silk hood. Coats in plaid and check were all the rage, especially over light summer dresses, and colour-coordinated satin hoods were an absolute must!

At the outbreak of war many horses were requisitioned for use by the military. One enterprising motor dealer, John Chilton & Co. of Old Hill, published a large advert headed 'War and the Commandeered Force' to sell new motor cars made by Ford, proclaiming that 'a Ford car will do the work of four horses – quicker, better, more efficiently'. Some sixty-five light and draft horses were requisitioned in Dudley and the fire brigade in Stourbridge lost four horses necessary for their use. Chief Officer Trow said that every effort would be made to effect a turnout when necessary but it was imperative to acquire a motor fire engine for the town. He stressed that without one, there would be delays in reaching fires in rural areas.

Manufacturing

Dudley Chamber of Commerce met on 11 August 1914 to consider the present trade outlook in a Special Meeting. They talked about 'carrying on of business during the somewhat abnormal conditions.' Advice was given about keeping people (especially warehousemen and clerks) in work; assisting the wives of those men fighting; seeking business in 'other directions'; continuing business as usual and not increasing food prices unnecessarily. As soon as war was declared all trade disputes ceased by mutual agreement; however, this did not last for long. Bank interest rates quickly increased to 10 per cent but this was short-lived and they soon fell back to 5 per cent.

Walsall Chamber kept a close eye on local activities. An early meeting of manufacturers was held; the outcome being that it was important to avoid unemployment. The Chamber promised to generate more local trade, partly by 'capturing' the enemy's trade. Further meetings were arranged to discuss this. Local manufacturer members of the Chamber were owed £50,000 by German and Austrian firms. There were restrictions placed on exports of saddles and harness; they could only be shipped abroad under special licence. This brought export trade to a halt and had long-term effects, especially in the USA which quickly filled the void and profited.

The manufacturing sector faced an uncertain future. Britain was heavily dependent on Germany before the war for many goods. Over half our sugar came from Germany; dye, especially for clothing; and cyanide were other commodities supplied mainly by the Germans and total trade was £80 million worth of imports and over £40 million in exports, almost a quarter of our total trade in Europe.

Raw material price rises were reported, causing a major problem for manufacturers. For example, leather prices rose because the price of raw hides increased significantly; many leather manufacturers relied on supplies from Bulgaria and Serbia. Boot manufacturers in Old Hill were directly affected, leading to increases in the price of boots, many of which were destined for the military. There were similar problems in Walsall, where manufacturers were expected to fulfil orders for the government to provide equipment for mounted troops.

In the galvanizing trade the cost of spelter (zinc) increased prohibitively. An interesting court case involved a charge of spelter theft at Stourbridge. Three months before the war began three men were arrested and a considerable quantity of spelter seized, suspected of being stolen. The application was for delivering up of the goods but two of the defendants were in Canada, having skipped bail. The applicant, Mr Mobberley, needed the metal which would have provided a week's work for his employees. The application was opposed by police as 'premature' and they informed the bench that positive

Victoria Leather Works, Old Hill.

First World War field kitchen equipment: many of the utensils for such operations were produced in the Black Country by companies such as Ernest Stevens (Judge brand) in Cradley Heath, as well as Izon's in West Bromwich.

identification of the spelter was not proved. The justices refused the application.

In Cradley Heath and Blackheath, as well as elsewhere, large quantities of German materials were used. Stoppage of supplies caused prices to rise alarmingly and affected the wages of puddlers. Similarly, the nut, bolt and chain industries were affected by the stoppage of supplies of raw material both from Germany and Belgium. Prices of pig-iron rose by as much as £1 to around £7 per ton. The glass trade also suffered, with many workers on short time; however, firms did their best to keep staff employed.

The news was not all bad. One Tipton firm secured a large order for pumps and a company in Dudley won a large order for engineering sections. These would have previously been filled by German companies. It was suggested there should be positive action to develop companies that previously operated in the shadow of their larger German counterparts.

The White Feather

The 'Order of the White Feather' was founded early in the war. Mainly young women were involved and they gave white feathers to young men not in uniform. This often caused anger and the government eventually had to distribute 'on war service' badges to those who were on essential war work but not in uniform. There were many examples of men whose lives were ruined by such practice, some leading to suicide. Women approached men asking for their lives and beseeching them to join the forces. If they refused, they were given this traditional badge of cowardice. One famous 'giving' to a man resulted in him using it to clean his pipe, remarking 'That's the second decoration I have received today; this morning the King gave me this', and showed the woman his Victoria Cross.

In September 1914 an appeal went out to young non-conformists who could fight to enlist immediately. This was a righteous and necessary conflict: 'a war against barbarians of the most evil and remorseless kind.' We were fighting for our very lives as a nation in a 'world war' and every man who could fight was wanted at once: 'For the Order of the White Feather there will soon be no room in our land.'

One man, Petty Officer Ernest Rogers from West Bromwich, was angry at the treatment meted out to his brother, who had tried to enlist but failed his medical. His response was: 'I shall be pleased to present with a bunch of fives anyone who presents him with a petticoat or a white feather.'

Joseph Bird was another West Bromwich man who had volunteered for active service but he had a weak chest and was almost blind in one eye. David Richards was his friend and had joined the army; he was a marksman and fought in France. David was home on leave and on a tram with Joseph; the former was recovering from wounds to his legs, having been shot twice. A young woman approached them on the tram and handed each one a white feather. Both grabbed the woman, put her across their laps and gave her the 'hiding of her life'. David went back to the front in early September 1916 and on his first day back on the front line he was killed in action with many of his colleagues. Joseph spent the war years helping servicemen, either at the District or Hallam hospitals. Many of the men he helped were people he knew from childhood.

Another example later in the war was William Weller, an architect from Wolverhampton. He was excused service for medical reasons and was also carrying out essential war work, building homes for steel workers. He received a letter containing a white feather. William's feather has been found, along with the letter, in the City Archive at Wolverhampton and has been displayed there. This is a very rare find as most men simply threw away the feather. The letter reads:

Sir

Your gallant and protracted defence against the brutal attacks of the local tribunal has been brought to the notice of the supreme council of the most notable order of The Trench Dodgers.

I am to inform you that the council have therefore, as a reward for your devotion to self regardless of narrow patriotism made you a companion of the said most noble order, the insignia of which is forwarded herewith.

I am Sir
Your Obedient Servant
A. Chicken Heart
Clerk to the Council

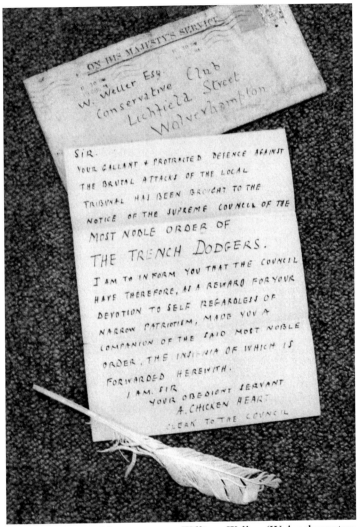

White feather and letter sent to William Weller. (Wolverhampton Archive)

To 'aid' recruitment some newspapers published a list of names of those men who had not volunteered, then later supplementary lists were published. Some individuals placed advertisements in the *County Express*, offering petticoats and white feathers to those who had refused to volunteer.

Life in difficult times

Food supply and demand was a constant problem for Britain. As the war progressed, rationing became necessary and inflation also caused many problems. The majority of these problems will be explored in the next chapter, 'Feeding the Black Country'.

Hop-picking at this time was a very popular holiday for Black Country families. The annual exodus from the Black Country often led to scuffles between families trying to claim carriages on special trains to Worcestershire and Herefordshire. As usual in 1914 these trains were swamped. There was a debate on hop-picking during a meeting of the Rowley Regis Federation Committee. School attendance officers raised the question of school holidays as 28 August would be the date when hop-pickers usually went away. Chairman Alfred Bassano believed it was worthwhile to start the holiday on this date to allow as much employment as possible. Others believed 4 September would be a better date to start and this was duly voted as the start date for the three-week holiday. Between 12 and 15 per cent of children in the borough went 'hoppen' with their families.

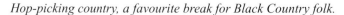

Hop-picking country, a favourite break for Black Country folk.

Motorists in the war were bound to be affected. Some 92,000 members of the AA nationally received a circular asking them to help the government, motorcyclists in particular being needed. The chairman of the AA saw the Under-Secretary for War and intimated that many AA members wished to place their cars and motorcycles at the disposal of the army and the circular sent to members talked about this likely offer. Any members prepared to help must send their details to the chairman at the AA offices in London so they could be classified and submitted to the War Office.

The announcement of war sparked a number of problems for tourists in Europe. Mr E.F. Dixon from Stourbridge was in Paris at the time, having left home on Saturday, 1 August. He returned safely to London, though he had lost part of his luggage. In a communication to Mrs Dixon he stated there was 'almost a panic amongst those desirous of returning to England.'

A lady from Clent, Miss E.R. Lee, and her friend had a thrilling escape from Germany. They were on their way to the Wagner Festival in Munich. They went via Harwich by ferry to the Hook of Holland and all seemed calm. The ladies boarded the train for Cologne, which was very busy as might be expected at this time of year. German soldiers were posted at the border into Germany and more en route to Mainz; they waved cheerily to the train as it passed. At their hotel in Frankfort (Frankfurt), the grim reality of events was made clear to them from newspapers. Russia was mobilizing, which meant that war was imminent; wherever they went they saw a sad, grave crowd.

The hotel was empty and foreign residents were leaving the town by every train. The ladies decided to try to return home and the British consul advised them to leave immediately but they could not escape before mobilization took place. Train services were still running but food was difficult to obtain; they were short of silver coin and notes were not easy to change. Finally they boarded a train for Cologne but their luggage was lost as it had gone straight to Munich. They reached the Belgian frontier en route to Ostend and had to leave the train and walk across the border. They then caught another train and eventually returned home safe and well.

Patriotism

Once war had been declared there was a wave of patriotism. The conflict was seen as a just cause and everything was done to ensure the British population was stirred into patriotic fervour. An American observer commented on the spirit of British men, and even more so British women, who were heard to say of their men: 'We can stand it if they go, but we could not stand it if they stayed at home.'

Local politicians were quick to come forward with messages of hope for their residents. Councillor Lench, Chair of Rowley Regis Urban District Council, encouraged people to keep a 'clear head and brave heart, honour the men who were giving their lives in the defence of liberty'. He made a request to only purchase sufficient food to service requirements. Patriotism of the highest order was encouraged across the Black Country. The Mayor of Wednesbury, Councillor Bishop, told his people that all would suffer and that victory was not without great sacrifice; he urged people to be courageous. He promised to care for the families of reservists who had been called up, especially in terms of providing food.

Wednesbury MP Sir John Norton-Griffiths encouraged the creation of a Home Defence Corps, to act in the event of invasion. Norton-Griffiths, nicknamed 'Empire Jack' for his violent and vulgar patriotism, was commissioned major having raised the 2nd King Edward's Horse at his own expense and he toured the trenches in a battered Rolls Royce loaded with fine wine.

Patriot funds were set up around the Black Country to supplement allowances made by the government to families of reservists and Territorials who had been called up. Many firms agreed to pay a proportion of the wages to their families of those employees who went to war. Harper, Sons & Bean from Tipton and Dudley was one example: they pledged 10 shillings a week until the men returned. Similarly, Tipton Education Committee agreed to pay 50 per cent of the salary of unmarried teachers who joined the army – partly as an incentive and partly to compensate their parents for the loss of family income – and to continue to pay increments to those teachers as if they had still been teaching.

A call to arms.

Concerts were staged around the Black Country and one example was at Wednesbury Town Hall in aid of the National Relief Fund. The ladies' choir chose stirring patriotic songs such as *England* and the *Hallelujah Chorus* and the mayor presided over the first concert. The following evening there was an open-air concert in Market Place, Wednesbury, given by the Crown Tube Works Prize Band.

In late September the Wesleyans, including those from Wednesbury and Darlaston, passed a resolution at their synod lamenting the fact that war had been forced on this country and recorded their horror of the war. However, the synod enthusiastically approved the grounds on which war was declared, to support Belgian neutrality and loyalty to France. They were also adamant there should be no peace until the military despotism of Germany and Austria was destroyed. They finally recognized the spirit of young Methodists who had enlisted in large numbers and urged all Christians to pray earnestly so that God may guide them in matters of supreme international importance that would arise for consideration when peace was proclaimed and to make future war impossible.

By October the Black Country had begun to receive Belgian refugees. The government indicated that refugees coming to our country were likely to be families, usually with at least one man; offers of hospitality should include accommodation for men. Ideally they should be in the same house but at the least in the same street or immediate area. Many were from poorer classes and mainly spoke French or Belgian. The first arrived in Wednesbury and West Bromwich, where great support was offered to them. Flags and bunting greeted the families who were provided with houses and food to support them. The refugees told graphic tales of the barbaric treatment suffered at the hands of the Germans.

The first refugees in Dudley arrived on 21 October; there were twenty-two in total. Others followed and a hostel was established in Castle Street. A second hostel in Old Cross Street was then opened to separate French- and Flemish-speaking Belgians because of friction between them.

October also saw insurance cover for damage by hostile craft such as the Zeppelin being offered. Initially premiums were high but they soon reduced because of the take-up of policies and the lack of claims. Premiums in coastal areas were higher than those in places like the Black Country.

Black Country hospitals

Within a week of the outbreak of war many Black Country hospitals were gearing up to accept wounded from the conflict. As the war progressed more use was made of hospitals in the region, causing great strain on resources as we will see later. Dudley Guest, Walsall Manor, Royal Hospital in Wolverhampton and Wordsley Hospital all accepted large numbers of wounded.

The committee of Walsall Hospital agreed with the Red Cross Society to place at least thirty beds at their disposal. To do this the hospital suspended plans to convert a ward for the use of children. Early in the conflict twenty-five wounded soldiers were moved to Dudley Guest Hospital, transferred from the Naval and Military Hospital in Portsmouth.

Christmas comes but once a year

Christmas and its symbols, such as holly and mistletoe, were seen as emblems of those social and domestic influences that continued to be important to people, despite so many having lost loved ones or being separated by war. Talk of merriment was seen as mockery and Christmas would not be the same throughout the duration of the war.

Dudley Guest Hospital, taken in 2011.

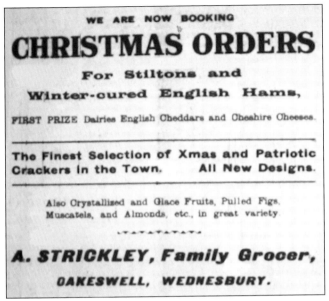

Despite food shortages and high prices, Christmas was still a time for celebration in 1914.

It was a time to reflect on the true meaning of Christmas, reinforced by the wave of generosity and unselfishness that had swept the country.

The Pope took steps to secure a Christmas truce but failed. According to a German source, Russia was the power that declined the truce. Reports stated that fighting on Christmas Day was not so severe and there were local truces, even football matches taking place between the German and British forces. A Walsall man, Private James Hughes, said the British were talking to the Germans and cigarettes were exchanged. Many soldiers were well looked after, with plenty of presents from home. However, fighting resumed as normal on Boxing Day and there was heavy shelling.

Children of servicemen were in the hearts and minds of local people. Children of those serving at the front received Christmas presents to give them a happy moment in this dark period. Such presents were purchased from the proceeds of funds set up for that purpose. Growing numbers of Belgian refugees were housed around the region. Some were resident at Moss Close in Walsall. Generous locals donated Christmas fare and provided entertainment on Christmas Day; even going so far as to hide the Christmas tree from the children. They were a persistent group of youngsters and, once they got wind of something happening, elected spies to see what was happening, which required 'sentries' to prevent 'infiltration'. On Christmas morning the refugees attended services at local churches, then returned to be confronted with roast goose, sausages, mince pies, fruit, tobacco and sweets. In the evening various entertainments took place, including musical chairs which required some explanation to the Belgians. The evening concluded with *God Save the King*.

Christmas at Walsall Workhouse and Infirmary was also bright and happy. Dining halls were decorated and a traditional roast beef dinner, followed by plum pudding, was served. The beef was accompanied by plenty of vegetables and washed down with beer and mineral water. After the meal, tobacco, fruit and sweets were served. A speech by Alderman Bull commented on the need for everyone to 'think and act righteously'. There was also reference to the response of the colonies, which showed that 'the sons of the Empire would not stand by and see the father thrashed'.

CHAPTER 3

Feeding the
Black Country

As the war progressed those left at home in the Black Country were almost as important as those fighting the conflict. Feeding the population became a real issue for the government and local authorities. Profiteering was both suspected and carried out and there were near-riots in many areas. Prices rose, even when government controls were imposed. Alcohol became a real issue: Black Country workers were traditionally heavy drinkers and beer had been, for generations, the safest drink because of poor water quality in the area. However, during the war government control was inevitable to maintain an efficient and productive workforce.

Panic-buying was actively discouraged and a letter was published by the Mayor of Wednesbury asking people not to believe rumours of what was happening abroad. He declared that buying too much food was unpatriotic and unwise. Patriotism by 'remaining calm and doing her duty' was the order of the moment for the housewife. Some shops closed temporarily and active discouragement was given to those stockpiling food. It was felt necessary to protect poorer people who didn't have the funds to stockpile food for an uncertain future.

By 15 August 1914 the government was considering legislation to prevent unreasonable withholding of foodstuffs. There had been cases around the country where there was great hardship, especially among the poor. The process of 'cornering' (the market) seems to have caused this. Wholesalers and producers were accused of holding back on

Marsh & Baxter advert from the early twentieth century.

supplying essential goods in the expectation that prices would rise, at which point they would release the goods and benefit from greater profits. This, along with panic-buying and the greed of the better-off who were able to stockpile food, contributed to the hardship. A rise in food prices was inevitable but this should have made food more plentiful because it would have attracted goods to Britain that would previously have gone to other markets.

The Board of Trade had powers to act if foodstuffs were being unreasonably withheld from the market. It could take possession of goods, for a reasonable price, and ensure their availability to the people. This Bill passed quickly through Parliament.

Marsh & Baxter Ltd of Brierley Hill were currently receiving their normal stock of pigs. Prices rose 25 shillings per pig once war was declared but by the following week prices had dropped back by 10s per pig. Despite this, Marsh & Baxter's retail price was held at pre-war levels, except for best bacon where prices rose a little. The company distributed 10,000 hams a day to re-supply wholesalers and these were packed at a rate of 1,000 an hour. Supply of pigs was for a time affected by farmers who refused to release stock, hoping that prices would rise.

Food supply was given plenty of coverage in newspapers: they speculated that prices would rise, eggs to 6d or 9d each! Eggs were likely to be the first product in short supply as they were imported in large numbers from the continent and the winter saw a reduction in supply. This encouraged British producers to keep hens in a more systemized way than on farms. The 'battery cage' system was still some way off; it developed in the early 1930s and grew at a greater pace after the Second World War. The year 1914 brought one of the finest yields of wheat in recent times, clearly an advantageous situation. In addition, Canada sent a million bags of flour to Britain. At Staffordshire Chamber of Agriculture the wheat supply for the future was debated. The war impacted on supply because Russia was one of the largest wheat producers and their supply would be disrupted. In Britain between 1880 and 1914 wheat acreage had halved from 3 million to 1.5 million, now a major problem and British farmers could not fulfil the demand.

In the early weeks of war across the Black Country there were public disturbances as people believed shopkeepers were cashing in on the situation and raising prices without justification. Disturbances occurred at Dudley Port and Quarry Bank, for example, with angry mobs out of control. Men and women were 'infuriated beyond control in consequence of the advanced prices of food stuffs' said one newspaper report. A shop in Dudley Port was looted, leading to arrests for theft and riot. Four men were committed for trial at Brierley Hill Quarter Sessions; magistrates warned that similar cases would be dealt with seriously.

The Dudley Port victim was Thomas Edward Smith of the Post Stores. During the incident damage was caused to baking ovens and flour was spilt. Smith stated he raised his prices because his suppliers raised theirs. He claimed police may have contributed to the situation because they did not move people on, implying sympathy with the protest. Mary Ann Harris (aged 36) and her son George (aged 14) were charged with theft of 14lb of flour and handling stolen goods; they were arrested at home and the flour was recovered. A few doors away 23-year-old John Thomas was arrested and charged with stealing a flitch of bacon from Smith; the bacon was also recovered. Thomas had previous convictions and was remanded in custody.

In Quarry Bank between 2,000 and 4,000 people gathered for a similar protest, threatening shop owners about prices. Two drunken men were arrested after they threatened to 'smash the shop' of Joseph Goodwin, a local councillor, over a 1½d dispute. Goodwin's shop was also looted, windows smashed and goods stolen; foodstuffs worth £100 were damaged. Arrests were made and Goodwin gave evidence of constant threats and stone-throwing. There were similar scenes in Netherton and Cradley Heath, keeping the police busy.

It was not all bad news though. Fereday's in High Street, Halesowen announced a new stock of chocolates and confections had arrived with over 150 varieties to choose from. They also announced supplies of biscuits and large quantities of tobacco, cigars, cigarettes and pipes. Prices, as well as the supply of foodstuffs, fluctuated wildly during this early period.

Throughout the war newspapers gave advice to housewives, including recipes and tips on economy. Manufacturers' adverts gave similar advice, such as Bird's Custard whose advert pointed out that eggs were expensive but Bird's Custard was cheap. The advert suggested serving hot custard with stewed prunes for a delightful treat.

One report from May 1915 declared flies a danger, being 'the most filthy of all filthy pests' which may prove more deadly than German poisonous shells and asphyxiating gas. It was feared that those flies currently causing disease in the trenches may, like the Zeppelins, cross the Channel and wreak havoc in Britain. The report described the life-cycle and habits of a fly and also where they bred most effectively, pointing out that a bald head was not the ideal place for a fly! The point was that without rubbish, there would be no flies. To assist the reader a lengthy list of 'rubbish' was printed, including 'animal internals', rhubarb leaves and fish heads. Fire was seen as the great purifier in this campaign. The diseases to be avoided were enteric fever, summer diarrhoea and diphtheria. This report covered the majority of a page in a broadsheet-sized newspaper.

The demon drink

Initially the government stance on drinking and alcohol was to declare it a local issue for authorities. It was said that 80 per cent of lost work time was because of drink, which was seen as an evil by Lloyd George: 'We are fighting Germany, Austria and drink, and as far as I can see the greatest of these three deadly foes is drink.' The Workers' Union believed the case against workers was exaggerated and opined that total prohibition would not solve the problem. Among their 1,800 local members, only two cases of neglect had been reported. King George unsheathed his sword against the dragon drink, according to headlines. It was a grave situation facing armament factories; he said he would give up drink and ban consumption in the Royal Household as an example. It was later reported that the Royal Table contained only barley water to drink. The 'King's Pledge' was taken by the Mayor of Wolverhampton, Alderman A. Baldwin Bantock. No consumption of alcohol took place at Bantock House during the war.

At the Walsall Brewster Sessions in February 1915, Chief Constable Thomson reported there were 157 alehouses, 78 beer houses and 33 off-licences selling beer. Including grocers and wine licences, there were 287 outlets for alcohol, one for every 321 head of population. Since 14 December 1914 premises had been closed between 6am and 9am following complaints that workmen were neglecting their duty and drinking in the morning. Police carefully supervised licensed premises and ensured that licence-holders generally conducted their houses satisfactorily. During 1914 255 people had been prosecuted for drink-related offences; up from 221 in 1913. Many were first-time offenders, possibly due to the excitement of the war. This pattern was repeated across the Black Country and newspaper articles on drink-associated cases were regular. One example was James Ryan, aged 40, charged with being drunk and disorderly in Park Street, Walsall. Ryan created a disturbance at the local recruiting office where he was being attested; the doctor refused to pass him and Ryan became abusive. Chief Constable Thomson stated that Ryan had thirty-eight previous convictions!

Board of Control restrictions on the sale of alcoholic liquor reduced the hours, previously 10am to 10pm, down to being open for five and a half hours each day. It was said a considerable section of the public was 'chafing under the conditions, but patriotism is their first consideration'. The restrictions made a difference; in Dudley a big decrease in drunkenness was reported. In 1912 there were 923 convictions in the county, in 1914 there were 683 and in 1915 there were 510. Drinking was mainly carried out among munitions workers, whose wages were good. Sir George Hingley of N. Hingley & Sons

Ltd said that high wages paid to munitions workers were scandalous and that this encouraged drinking. A large number of registered clubs closed as the war progressed for want of members. In 1915 it was disclosed in Parliament that drunkenness had fallen nationally by 50 per cent and in the Midlands by 60 per cent. This was said to be because of restrictions on liquor traffic by the Central Control Board.

Despite regulations from the Board of Control, it was apparent that some public houses were selling beer cheaply. This was so-called 'thin' beer, sold at 2d per pint, causing unfair competition among publicans. One theory was that it would help to reduce drunkenness because it was weaker but no decision was made about what action could or should be taken. In June 1917 'light beer', only 2 per cent proof, 'almost a non-intoxicating drink', was sold officially in works' canteens without an excise licence. One benefit was that it was much cheaper than 'ordinary' beer and cost about 2d a pint, which still included a profit for the canteen.

Beer was important for some workers. At around the same time as the introduction of 'light beer' Sedgley ironworkers were unable to get their beer due to shortages and had to stop working because of a lack of fluid. The beer shortage was due to a lack of hops in the latter years of the war. This was a government decision, partly to assist in a more general way by reducing the amount of barley and sugar used by brewers so those items could be used to feed the nation instead.

A Temperance Society message in 1918 was that £5 12s 7d had been spent on alcohol in the previous year per head of population. This equated to £518,000 in a town the size of Walsall and could have purchased 200 aeroplanes or five submarines.

There were lighter moments among the horrific war news. Newspapers such as the *Tipton Herald* published columns on 'House and Home'. In January 1916 the humble parsnip was featured with recipes such as creamed parsnips, parsnip soup, parsnip croquettes and one that took my eye: 'parsnips in disguise'. This involved boiling parsnips and mixing them with white sauce, seasoned with salt and pepper. I doubt many Black Country children were fooled by this disguise! There was also a recipe for parsnip pudding with lemon sauce but the less said about that the better, unless you are a great fan of parsnips.

The 'interesting' parsnip recipes may have been related to another piece of news in the same paper. Mr Woodward of Gospel End, Sedgley sold two gigantic parsnips he had grown for a total of 14 shillings. The use of starchy vegetables such as parsnips, beets and carrots was enthusiastically encouraged by nutritionists, local authorities and the government. They were a good source of energy, easy to grow and provided more nutritional value than something like celery, for example.

Levity aside, far-reaching measures had been taken by the government to ensure the national food supply. For example, much of our beet sugar previously came from Germany and the government immediately made arrangements to purchase cane sugar world-wide to replace this shortfall. Early in the war the government also requisitioned the whole supply of frozen meat from Australasia, mainly for consumption by the army.

In January 1916 a new canteen was opened at Harper, Sons & Bean, Dudley, at their Waddam's Pool site which had become one of the largest munitions factories in the region. This was in line with other similar operations around the country and was staffed by the YMCA and YWCA. It opened to 'keep up the vitality of the workers.' A spokesman for the YMCA said that this was the best facility in the country and had been provided entirely by the company. Some 120 Dudley ladies worked as volunteers to run the canteen. Men and women were segregated when dining, as were the office staff who had a separate dining room. Waiting staff, the volunteers, wore a purple uniform. There were two hot meals and two puddings to choose from and sittings were at midday and midnight, with other services available around the clock.

By February 1916 government regulations on keeping pigs was relaxed because of the war. In the nineteenth century many Black Country families kept pigs but a drive to improve sanitary conditions in order to eradicate diseases like cholera led to strict rules being imposed. This meant that pig-keeping in most Black Country households stopped. There were problems for pig-keepers; inflation meant it was almost prohibitively expensive to buy feed for pigs. Yes, they could use food waste but there was already advice for housewives on utilizing excess food.

In April 1916 bread was in short supply and housewives were recommended to bake their own. A recipe was published: for every 1lb of flour add 2tsp Berwick's baking powder and salt, then thoroughly mix these dry ingredients before gradually pouring on ½pint cold water, or milk and water, then mix thoroughly into a dough. Yes, this was an advertisement disguised as an article, common practice for newspapers.

By December 1916 food supply difficulties were of serious concern. British residents already had food consumption regulated by high prices and further regulation was not seen as effective. The cost of such regulation outweighed the benefits and caused irritation; increased supplies were seen as the only way forward. Earlier in May 1916 came reports of shops closing early due to lack of labour and difficulty in obtaining supplies. This position worsened and 1917 saw early-closing orders imposed. This did not apply to canteens situated near works that were kept open for the workers. Similarly, railways were exempted from selling restrictions, as were bazaars or sales of work for charitable purposes and other non-profit events.

In February 1917 Stourbridge publishing house Mark & Moody advertised in the *County Express* newspaper the publication of the fourth edition of 'Puddings Which Require One Egg'. In the same newspaper one housewife, also a mother of three children, commented on her allocation of rations. She claimed the food ration was just about adequate but that she had to run her house on 'most economical lines'. Her family could just about cope on the ration of meat which included bacon for breakfast but bread was trickier. She said she would probably not cope if her husband was at home as he required a good deal more bread to be fit for work. She also advocated putting the children first, as it was beneficial for adults to lose a little superfluous body fat!

In May 1917 Dudley Council were warned by their Mayor, Thomas Chambers, about the grave situation of food shortages. This situation was exacerbated by U-boats that had sunk many cargo vessels. Chambers urged a message about reducing waste; the ordinary man and woman were not good at re-using 'scraps or leftovers', he said. One suggestion was for those who drank whisky with milk to drop the milk and give it to their children. Also the lunchtime snack of a cheese sandwich with the midday glass of beer should be dispensed with, although presumably the beer was still allowed! These suggestions were put forward to avoid 'the horrible phantom of starvation stalking over the land'. A suggested remedy in nearby Tipton was to sell

Haybox.

families only the correct quantity of food for their needs. This was not long before rationing was introduced, so maybe the suggestion came about through insider knowledge!

At the same time radical gardening advice was given about growing celery in a small garden plot: people should grow food, not luxuries, wrote the correspondent. Celery was low in nutrition and should be dispensed with as it took up too much space, used too much manure and occupied the ground for too long. It was not comparable in food value to beetroot, for example. It is a fact that celery is the only salad crop that uses up more calories in the process of being eaten than it supplies, so maybe the writer had a point!

To help women and mothers, cookery schools opened. There were five in Dudley, where lectures were given and discussions held on housekeeping. Elsewhere 'food economy shops' opened. Their objective was to reduce consumption and eliminate waste. Later in the war, fuel economy led to women using hayboxes to complete the cooking of partially-cooked foods.

By August 1917 food rationing was the reality. Plans to ration sugar were drawn up; not because of significantly reduced supply but to ensure that everyone had equal access. It was estimated there was enough sugar for everyone in Britain to have half a pound each per week. The problem was that our population had grown during the war years but coastal areas had lost population, causing an imbalance between supply and demand by area.

A better and cheaper supply of saccharine was promised to supplement sugar. It was recommended for many uses, including diabetics, and could also be used in cooking. However, it was not suitable for children who required the calories provided by sugar. Saccharine was sold in tablet form and a Walsall chemist, Messrs Haywards, reportedly made the best, at least according to their advert.

The following month fruit-growers were told that they could buy limited quantities of preserving sugar for jam. This offer was not available to anyone else. It was limited to half a pound per 1lb of fruit grown for jam. Application was needed in writing, stating the quantity of fruit and the amount of sugar required.

In January 1918 afternoon tea was banned by the Food Control Committee. This was due to shortage of supplies and an appeal was made to see it discontinued as soon as possible. Warning of meat supply shortage was also given, as even the 'emergency' supply of tinned meat in Walsall was not sufficient according to their local Food Control Committee.

Rationing

At the start of 1918 ration cards were distributed. Traders were asked to send details of tea, butter and margarine stocks to the Food Control Committee. Ration cards were tied to a specific retailer and could only be transferred to another shop once they had run out. The committee could transfer cards if they believed that a particular retailer had too many customers.

A standby cache of three days' supply was created. It was forecast that some people would complain about the system but the war required personal sacrifice from everyone; there had to be a balance between giving the people enough and not running out. However, just having a

MEAT CARD [L. and H. C.]

Office of Issue *Kensington*

A. Holder's Name

Address:—

B. Holder's Signature:—
Ethel Isabel Wilson

C. Butcher's Name and Address:—

IF FOUND, DROP IN A PILLAR BOX.

Meat ration card (1918).

ration card was no guarantee that there would be sufficient supply; shortages could still happen.

In February meat supply in the Black Country was again of concern; twenty-five cases of rabbits had been sent to Walsall by the Ministry of Food, together with twenty-five quarters of beef to add to the regular weekly supply. Meat was not currently rationed but national plans were currently being drawn up. Horse meat had been tried by about thirty people at the Town Hall and found to be acceptable. A sample was ordered for the next Food Control Committee meeting. Other measures included retaining the supply of tripe locally and no longer sending part of it elsewhere and redistributing pork from pork butchers to beef and mutton butchers to reduce queuing. In March it was reported that meat rationing would start nationally in early April 1918.

In April 1918 boys aged between 13 and 18 received a supplementary ration of meat; similarly additional rations for 'arduous workers' were increased. In May the definition of 'arduous work' caused anomalies. A postman qualified but a postwoman did not! In fact, few women qualified at all. Adolescents faced similar problems between the sexes with distinctions made between boys and girls.

Lard also became subject to rationing in July 1918. It was noted, however, that our total ration of fat was four times that of Germany, which only allotted 2oz per person per week.

Black Country allotment-holders and fruit-growers were urged to grow more rhubarb. Their crop could be sold to a company to be made into jam and the bulk of that jam would go back to the area providing the rhubarb. In July 1918 jam joined the list of rationed goods, with an allocation of 8oz per person per week. Soldiers at the front were supplied with plenty of jam; in fact it was reported that some men were 'fed up' with having too much.

In September 1918, with Christmas less than four months away, it was announced that Christmas puddings for the troops would be supplied by the British army and relatives were requested not to send puddings to their loved ones. The practice of sending puddings to the front was common throughout the war. Presumably this change was to assist the Post Office, feed the troops more effectively and preserve ingredients for consumption at home.

CHAPTER 4

1915:
Deepening Conflict

Timeline of events

- 19 January: First Zeppelin raid on England
- 18 February: German submarine blockade of Great Britain begins
- 1 March: Britain and France sign joint declaration to prevent trade by or with Germany
- 10 March: Battle of Neuve Chapelle begins
- 22 April: Battle of Ypres (1915) begins, ends on 23 May; first German gas cloud attack on Western Front
- 7 May: SS *Lusitania* sunk by German submarine *U-20*
- 23 May: Italian government orders mobilization and declares war against Austria
- 31 May: First German airship raid on London
- 7 June: German airship LZ37 destroyed mid-air near Ghent (first successful attack by aeroplane)
- 2 July: Munitions of War Act becomes law in Britain; Ministry of Munitions formed
- 25 September: Allied Autumn Offensive begins; Battle of Loos starts
- 30 September: Lord Derby assumes control of recruiting in Britain
- 13 October: Most severe airship raid on East Coast and London with 200 casualties
- 10 November: Requisitioning Committee formed in Britain; order authorizes requisition of ships for carriage of foodstuffs

By the start of 1915 it was clear that the conflict was not going to be concluded quickly. There was speculation about where the major battles and fronts would be located, and the Germans were employing new tactics such as Zeppelins and submarine blockades. The system of awarding military contracts to companies around the region was becoming unworkable and recruitment into the forces was slowing down everywhere. As the year progressed, a serious threat to the war effort came in the shape of a serious shell shortage.

The horrors of war began to emerge. During March reports were published of the Battle of Ypres in October 1914. The headline read: 'Fifteen survivors of a party of one hundred and fifty'. These were men from the 1st South Staffordshire Regiment, sent to reinforce the Warwickshire Regiment. Only fifteen out of 150 got through safely. There were also graphic descriptions of wounded men in the report. Reports such as these were starting to filter back to those left at home; names of the dead and wounded made reports very personal to the local population.

YES, AN' THE OLE KISER — I BET 'E AINT OUT ON A NIGHT LIKE THIS !!

Postcard sent from the front in February 1915.

Reports from the front were sometimes inaccurate. Private John Worley was reported to have been found dead on the battlefield; however, his parents were overjoyed to receive a letter from him saying he had been wounded during a bayonet charge at Ypres on 13 May. This was not the only case as Sergeant William Nock, a well-known local boxer, had also denied reports of his own death reported some weeks earlier. One sad case of a misreported death was Sergeant William Mallaband, wrongly reported dead in November 1914 but actually killed on 18 May 1915. A career soldier, Mallaband had served twenty-one years with the colours, twelve of them in India, and was an accomplished athlete.

There were many examples of patriotism and also of sacrifices made by Black Country families. In some cases four or five sons were fighting at the front and some examples were published in newspapers to encourage more men to join up. There were constant fund-raising events for war-related charities. One innovative idea was the collection of eggs for wounded soldiers which commenced in August 1915. It became the National Egg Collection for the Wounded. Children in Black Country schools regularly took part in 'egg days', collecting and despatching them for wounded men. Egg-collection continued throughout the war. It was estimated that 200,000 eggs were needed each week and 10,000 eggs per day were shipped to hospitals in France. A film was also made to celebrate it, *From Hen to Hospital*, to help support the national egg-collection movement. By 1918 there was a serious national egg shortage; many people had got rid of their chickens, thinking they could not get food for them because of general shortages. This 'blip' was overcome and by the end of the war over 40 million eggs had been collected and distributed.

The New Year in Walsall was marked by a party for service children. A number of presents had been sent to the town by children of Americans and these were distributed at the party. For most children the event was a happy one, with Punch and Judy and conjurers providing entertainment, enjoyed by children and mothers alike. About 4,000 people attended. There were 550 presents allocated to Walsall for this party, not enough for all the children of the 736 fathers at the front. The mayor and mayoress (Alderman and Mrs J.N. Cotterell) led a local committee to provide presents for all 2,554 of the local children, as well as forty-four Belgian children living in Walsall. For one little girl who saw a number of soldiers at the entrance it was not such a happy occasion. She made her way towards the soldiers. When asked where she was going, she replied: 'I want to ask the soldiers where my daddy is.' She was a war orphan.

The motor vehicle had emerged as a new form of transport in the late-nineteenth century and the Black Country was quick to get involved in production and development. This war was probably the first where motor transport in all its emerging forms was widely used. In early January advertisements appeared for motor drivers (car and petrol lorries) required for mechanical transport with the Army Service Corps. The men would enlist for the period of the war; pay was 6 shillings a day with a separate allowance if married. Recruitment took place on 13 January at Whittington Barracks. Candidates required

The Black Country was a large producer of motor vehicles during the war. Star at Wolverhampton made large numbers of cars and commercial vehicles similar to the one depicted here.

testimonials showing their driving experience and those successful were required to proceed to the Mechanical Transport Depot the following day.

Policing

By the end of 1914 duties of police officers had changed vastly from the normality that existed before the war. The number of police officers was increased by the formation of two Police Reserve forces, the first from ex-servicemen and police officers and the second by swearing in Special Constables. By the New Year, nationally there were 120,000 Special Constables serving or ready to serve, compared with about 35,000 regular officers (outside London). Many of these extra resources were put into roles such as keeping observation of criminal suspects and preventing offences under the Defence of the Realm Act, as well as protecting public works. They were also employed in administering the requirements of the Aliens Restriction Act. Many Specials put their motor vehicles, cycles and horses at the disposal of the police. At this time the police in Walsall also had responsibility for the fire brigade, which comprised a chief officer, two inspectors, two sergeants and twelve constables.

It was mid-December 1915 before Special Constables gave evidence in court and the first case was reported extensively because of this. It involved a straightforward drunk and disorderly incident at The Delph, Brierley Hill. The authorities felt that an important point needed to be made about informing the public exactly what powers the Special Constables possessed. Superintendent Johnson prosecuted the case and remarked that the force had been depleted because of the war and the public needed to know that Specials 'were not to be treated as toys to be played with'. The court was told that when they were on duty and wearing their armbands, they had as much power as ordinary policemen.

Special Constabulary Long Service Medal, instituted by the king in 1919, for those 'Specials' who carried out faithful and devoted service during the war. It was awarded only to those who had served three years and performed a minimum of 150 duties.

Dudley Council decided that the borough would take over the contract of its own police. This would enable them to retain their fire service, whereas to go with either Worcestershire or Staffordshire County would require the formation of a voluntary fire service. The suggestion that a locally-appointed Watch Committee would be influenced in their decision-making and possibly become corrupt was refuted. Wolverhampton was another town with its own borough police force; it had been part of Staffordshire Police but then decided to return to being a borough force. By the early 1900s the Wolverhampton force numbered over 100 officers. During the war both Wolverhampton and Walsall employed women police officers.

Assistance for soldiers' wives and mothers was provided for in some areas by 'Tipperary Rooms'. One of these opened in Upper Bridge Street, Walsall in February. By this time there were some fifty such rooms around the country but this was the first in the Black Country. Eva Lowry made a plea for donations of money, personal services and furniture to help set up the house. The rooms were to be used as club rooms, tea rooms and play rooms. By mid-March the facility opened, including a well-fitted nursery where children were looked after while their mothers relaxed. An army of volunteers signed up to carry out the arrangements. The rooms were open daily from 2pm to 9pm. By mid-June the ones in Walsall had been open for three months. They were being used by 261 members from across the borough and offered support such as a savings bank, sewing class and a register of members seeking day employment. There were lectures on Tuesdays and the nursery was open every afternoon.

Working pay and conditions

Inflation continued to be a problem. Food prices rose almost weekly and supply was also an issue. Utility services, such as the gas supply, were becoming a problem. This was an emerging industry and local authorities had taken on the role of supplying to businesses and householders. More gas was being used; a good thing but this had an impact on the infrastructure and more money needed to be invested in storage (retorts). The gas was produced from coal and again, with increased demand for and cost of coal, large price increases were inevitable.

As the war progressed, greater demands were placed on the workforce in the Black Country which eventually began to look like one huge munitions factory. More jobs were opened up for women but in some cases women were paid only half the pay of a man doing similar work. This prompted intervention from organizations such as the National Federation of Women Workers who arranged public meetings and encouraged women to join so that better conditions could be achieved. Women had to meet the same increases in the cost of living as men and by March 1915 food prices had risen by 33 per cent compared to pre-war prices.

Well-known union activist Charles Sitch from Cradley Heath addressed a meeting, stating that conditions for women in the Midlands were the worst in the country. He cited Lancashire women workers who received the same rates of pay as men. He reminded the meeting of what had been achieved during the Women Chainmakers' Strike of 1909 which led to a minimum wage of 12s a week, the first minimum wage to be introduced in the country. Women workers elsewhere had applied to employers to advance wages to meet the increased cost of food and so far there had not been a single refusal. A number of women present said that they would be sacked if they joined the society. This was robustly countered: the federation had a legal advice bureau and the men were with the women regarding equal rights. The meeting ended with a resolution approving the principles of trade unionism and pledging those present to join the local branch of the federation or another kindred organization and to persuade others to do the same.

Despite early suspension of trade disputes, strikes became commonplace during the war. Some were threatened and led to pay increases, while others took place, disrupting essential war work. In April leather workers threatened strike action for a pay rise. These were workers making materials for gun teams: their pay had been agreed in October 1914 but the deal had not been honoured. The case was referred to Sir George Askwith and the Disputes Board at the Board of Trade; during their deliberations workers agreed to carry on working. The dispute had not been resolved by the end of May, with women being most affected as they were sometimes earning only a quarter the rate of men, despite 520 women now being members of the Midland Leather Trades Federation. Finally, in June 1915 Askwith announced his decision. The Disputes Board reaffirmed that they thought the wages were fair and after a meeting between Sir George and the affected men, they loyally accepted the decision.

In June the Ministry of Munitions was formed and took over all arrangements relating to employment and work of this nature. Locally a War Munitions Committee was formed in conjunction with the Traders' Association. Birmingham was made the centre for this area and Black Country Chambers of Commerce were urged to work closely with the Birmingham committee. In July the Munitions of War Act 1915 brought private companies supplying the armed forces under the tight control of the Ministry of Munitions which regulated wages, hours and employment conditions. It was a penal offence for a worker to leave his current job at such a 'Controlled Establishment' without his employer's consent, which in practice was almost impossible to obtain. This followed the 'Shell Crisis' when supplies of material to the front became a political issue.

The shell crisis of 1915 was a shortage of artillery shells on the front lines that led to a political crisis. It was argued that strategic plans caused over-reliance on shrapnel to attack infantry in the open, which caused a shortage of high-explosive shells in most major armies. At

Various shells and casings: 1 and 3 are shrapnel shells; 2 is a common shell. The lower variants are filled and were designated by a red band.

the start of the war it was believed that heavy guns alone could control the battlefield. Because of stable lines on the Western Front, it was easy to build railway lines to deliver all the shells that could be produced. The crisis emerged in 1915 because the high rate of fire over long periods led to the stock of shells becoming depleted; a serious problem since autumn 1914. The British Commander-in-Chief Field Marshal Sir John French gave an interview to *The Times* in March, calling for more ammunition. Lord Northcliffe, owner of *The Times* and the *Daily Mail*, blamed Lord Kitchener (Secretary of State for War) for the recent death in action of his nephew. In April Prime Minister Asquith stated that the army had sufficient ammunition. On 14 May *The Times* published the messages: 'Need for shells: British attacks checked: Limited supply the cause: A Lesson from France … want of an unlimited supply of high explosives was a fatal bar to our success.' This clearly pointed the finger of blame at the government.

The crisis contributed to weakening public appreciation of the government and was a significant factor in the fall of the Liberal government. A coalition was formed, leading to the rise to power of David Lloyd George as Minister of Munitions, eventually replacing Asquith as prime minister in December 1916. This crisis showed that the country was not on a full war footing and with talk of the 'big push' being made regularly, men on the front line had to be suitably equipped.

The whole economy needed to be geared for war if the allies were to prevail in France. Suppliers and factories in Commonwealth countries, particularly Canada, were reorganized under the Imperial Munitions Board to improve supplies of shells and other essentials. The Health of Munitions Workers Committee, one of the first investigations into occupational health and safety, was set up in 1916 to improve productivity in factories.

The National Projectile Factory

This massive works was erected in 1915 for production of artillery shells in the build-up to the big push on the Somme in 1916. Land was purchased at Waddams Pool, Dudley from Messrs Harper & Bean (the Bean Car manufacturers). After the war the factory was sold to the Co-operative, who used it to manufacture hollowware. The factory was purpose-built and authorized by the Ministry of Munitions in August 1915, construction being completed in May 1916. It was managed by George Bean, Chairman of A. Harper, Sons & Bean who had their own munitions factory but could not themselves produce enough to meet demand. By November 1916 the plant was producing 21,000 shell casings per week. The factory prompted the following local refrain:

The façade of the Bean factory; all that remains today of what was originally a grand entrance.

I haven't been a soldier
Or fought for King or Queen
But I've been wounded by shot and shell
At Harper, Sons and Bean

The factory originally employed around 4,000 workers, many of whom were women (munitionettes) and children. A huge influx of people into the region caused serious housing problems and houses were built at Brewery Fields for the workers to live in. These had to be demolished in the 1930s as being too dangerous to live in.

From September 1916 the factory produced 6″, 18lb and 60lb shrapnel shells, progressing to the manufacture of 6″ chemical shells in 1917. In late 1916 the government appealed for more women to join the workforce and offered free training in aspects of munitions manufacture. The hours varied but pay was generally good, although the work could sometimes be dangerous, dealing with chemicals and high explosives. Gun repair was also undertaken in 1917. Eventually, production of chemical shells overtook production of shrapnel. A steel shortage in March 1918 meant production changed, for a time, to aero engines. However, the National Projectile Factory continued making shells until the end of the war. Part of the building still stands in Hall Street, Dudley.

Recruitment
Efforts to recruit men for service continued to falter in April. Captain Wheeler, Secretary of the Territorial Force Association, visited district recruitment committees to urge them to consider house-to-house canvassing. This was a large undertaking and there were press appeals for volunteers to assist. Previously less 'intrusive' measures had been used but these were not supplying sufficient men for the front. This new proposal was in effect a mini-census, ascertaining how many men were eligible to be enlisted in each household and asking why they had not yet signed up. It was suggested at this time that women could work as conductresses on the tram networks to free up further men to enlist. Young men were still regularly operating trams and one commentator said it was strange for the tram company to have replaced enlisted men with other young men. The call was for more women to work on the trams, although this was greeted with horror in some areas.

It was felt that essential war work was being held up because many men employed in that work had enlisted. The War Office view was that equipment was as important as men, therefore some workers were refused leave to enlist in the forces, principally those making munitions.

By the end of April the likelihood of conscription came closer with a report that said within three months ALL men of military age would be required for military purposes. The War Office recommended that women should be trained in leather-stitching in Walsall and the local Board of Trade and Education Committee immediately set to the task, using old offices in Bradford Street. A committee was appointed to set up the workroom and it was agreed that twenty women at a time could be trained with this being for a minimum of one month.

In June 1915 Australia's *Sydney Daily Telegraph* reported weekly enlistment of 1,500 men, compared with eighteen in Walsall for the week. It was also noted that recently 70,000 Englishmen had been to watch a football match and the Australians could not fathom out why this was the case. It was also said that 900 Australian rugby players had enlisted and in New Zealand, the home of rugby, they could not field a team as all the men had gone to the front. This was not the first criticism involving footballers and football fans. Role models from sport were needed: men such as Walsall cricketer Walter Henry Cox, who showed great promise in his chosen sport. He received a commission in August 1914 in the South Staffordshire Regiment aged 19 and in April 1915 was promoted to lieutenant. Cox was killed in action on 16 June 1915 by a shell that also killed three other men. He was the first of Walsall's

BLACK CAT
CIGARETTES

PREPARATION OF
SOLDIERS' DINNERS

Cigarette card depicting women preparing soldiers' dinners. Many women volunteered for overseas service, mainly in France and Belgium, working in kitchens but also as nurses and in other roles.

twenty or so players who had enlisted to be killed in action. A Football Battalion was formed in December 1914; by March 1915 122 professional footballers had joined and it was deployed to the front in January 1916.

Around the Black Country, just as elsewhere, recruitment had stagnated. Despite impassioned pleas, stirring speeches and recruitment events, not enough men were signing up.

Recruitment was not limited solely to the army and navy. Many doctors, nurses and other professionals were called up or asked to volunteer. In April thirteen ladies from the Bloxwich Red Cross Voluntary Aid Detachment had been selected for service in military hospitals. They passed interviews in London and were now available to be called upon at twenty-four hours' notice. They signed up for twelve months' service, which could mean deployment on the Continent. Nationally, Staffordshire and Somerset had given the best response to this appeal. Early in May 1915 it was reported that three of the ladies had received their telegrams informing them that they were going to France.

Lord Derby's Group Recruiting Scheme

On 11 October 1915 Lord Derby was appointed Director General of Recruiting. He brought forward a programme five days later, often called the Derby Scheme although its official title was the 'Group Scheme', for raising the numbers of recruits. Men aged 18 to 40 were informed that under the scheme they could continue to enlist voluntarily or attest with an obligation to come if called up later on. The War Office notified the public that voluntary enlistment would soon cease and that the last day of registration would be 15 December 1915.

Lord Derby (Edward George Villiers Stanley), Director General of Recruiting in 1915.

Men accepted for service who had attested under the Derby Scheme could choose to defer joining up and were designated as 'Class A'. Those who agreed to immediate service were placed in 'Class B'. 'Class A' men were paid a day's army pay for the day they attested and given a grey armband with a red crown as a sign they had volunteered. The men were officially transferred into Section B of the Army Reserve and sent back to their homes and jobs until called up. Men who attested under this part of the Derby Scheme were classified into married and single status and into twenty-three groups organized by age. We will read more about the scheme and its effect on recruitment in the chapter titled 'The Realization'.

Christmas 1915

Across the Black Country people remembered loved ones who were either serving overseas or who were being held as prisoners of war. Charity collections raised funds to send parcels to the men. One example was Dudley Patriotic Committee, which made a plea for food and clothing for the thirty or so Dudley workers currently being held as prisoners of war in Germany and Constantinople. The committee arranged to send every man a large parcel every other Monday and the plea was for workers to collect items so that this could continue.

Servicemen wounded and recovering in England were also remembered. In December there were 155 wounded soldiers at Dudley Guest Hospital and an appeal was launched to raise funds to give them every possible comfort over the Christmas period.

Other well-intentioned causes included sending items to the men at the front and those on board naval vessels. A regular national call was made for people to send old books and magazines for British servicemen to satisfy their demand for literature. This was especially poignant for sailors keeping a lonely vigil in the North Sea. It was forecast that across all fronts 100,000 items were required to supply all servicemen but only about half this number was currently being supplied. Other items requested included footballs, mouth organs and tobacco. Staff and workers at H. Marlow's Excelsior Works in Dudley collected money and sent pipes, tobacco, cigars and cigarettes to their work colleagues serving with the army to show they had not been forgotten. In January 1916 almost 300 acknowledgements had been received from Brierley Hill soldiers for presents sent to them by the local Christmas Gifts Committee.

Preparations for Christmas continued amidst war work in the Black Country. People were informed that for the five days before Christmas Day they could purchase spirits between the hours of 11.30am and

5.30pm. Wines, ales and the like could be purchased from 11.30am to 8.30pm. Sales were being controlled by the Defence of the Realm Act and the notice was contained in an advert for Rutland and Lett, Wine and Spirit Merchants, High Street, Dudley. Money was actually plentiful, with increased wages, war allowances and almost unlimited overtime, so there was no shortage of cash. People spent freely, having had a year of 'unexampled prosperity'.

Thursday, 23 December was a memorable one for the children of Dudley and Woodside soldiers: 2,300 were entertained in The Empire and the Public Halls, with the mayor and mayoress in attendance. 'Appropriate and seasonable pictures' were shown and each child was given a bag containing a piece of cake, a bun, a mince pie, an orange and some sweets. Similarly, residents in Tipton Green and Park Ward, Tipton raised funds for a Christmas party for soldiers' children. It was not all good news though, as the annual old folks' Christmas dinner at Pensnett was cancelled because of the war.

Christmas Day 1915 was very much a 'stay-at-home' one. Transport was difficult because the tramcars had been stopped, the result of a ballot of tram drivers. The shadow of the Great War was over everyone, diminishing people's appetite for social pleasure. The weather was rainy and windy, a so-called 'Green Christmas', which folklore decrees is a prolific way of filling the churchyard.

The Christmas message from the Dudley mayor's parlour was:

'When Victory's Signal flashes through the skies
But – until then – welcome the fiercest fray
We fight for freedom God gives us "The Day".' (Marie Corelli)

Boxing Day storms
On Boxing Day the nation experienced one of the worst gales for twenty years. At 4pm chimney pots were blown away and roofs lifted from buildings in what was described as almost a whirlwind. Dudley and Kate's Hill bore the brunt due to being among the highest areas in the region, with much damage reported. One man in Kate's Hill, recovering from pneumonia, had his roof blown right in. He was quickly taken to the infirmary by police ambulance. Many lucky escapes were reported across the region and, no doubt, builders were kept busy for some time after the storm.

The gale caused considerable damage to property in Wolverhampton. In Tettenhall trees were blown down; similarly trees were blown down on the road past Baggeridge and blocked traffic. At Tipton a youth and a horse were both injured when a cowshed blew down. The whole country reported problems, from Swansea right up to Aberdeen. The storms and blizzards damaged telephone lines; these took time to repair and a report as late as April said one subscriber tried to telephone Brierley Hill all morning and had to give it up. He could have travelled by tram and back three times during the time he spent trying to make contact.

So 1915 went out with a bang but the first month of 1916 would leave a more lasting impression on the people of the Black Country ...

CHAPTER 5

Zeppelin Raids
over the Black Country

❖

The events of the night of 31 January 1916 rocked the Black Country and changed life for the rest of the war. Thought by many to be safe from Zeppelins, this night's events shattered that illusion and impacted on everyone. Ironically the Black Country was not the intended target but weather and other factors conspired and created a night of death, destruction and fear; fear that continued throughout the remainder of the war.

The threat of invasion or bombardment from the air was not new for Great Britain. In 1794 balloons had been developed with the

Zeppelin.

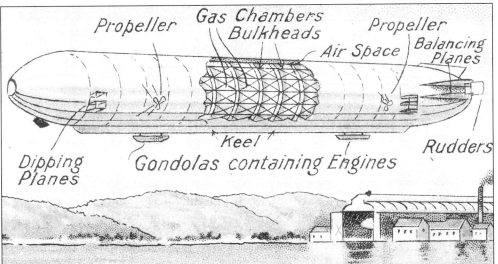

Propeller   Gas Chambers   Propeller
Bulkheads
Air Space   Balancing Planes
Dipping Planes   Keel   Gondolas containing Engines   Rudders

intention of using them in wartime. France set up a balloon corps, the Aérostiers, and used them during their conflict with Austria for aerial reconnaissance. They were later used against the British at the Battle of Aboukir during Napoleon's Egyptian campaign. At this battle the balloons were destroyed by the British and Napoleon disbanded them on his return to France in 1799. This removed the threat of aerial invasion from across the English Channel. Better use was made of military balloons during the American Civil War but still only for reconnaissance purposes.

The British experimented with balloon technology for reconnaissance between 1862 and 1871 and balloons were actively deployed in the Second Boer War (1899–1902), principally during the Siege of Ladysmith. Germany was able to use its Zeppelins for more than reconnaissance by reducing the weight of the airship and overcoming earlier technology's weight restrictions, thereby allowing them to carry bombs and other weapons.

Count Ferdinand von Zeppelin was the man who made the first models in 1899 and by 1914 twenty-one Zeppelin airships had been manufactured, used both for reconnaissance and for aerial bombardment. The first mention of their use in the war was at the end of August 1914 over Antwerp and they were first used against targets in Britain in January and April 1915 over East Anglia. In June 1915 Zeppelins were reported over London and some ninety bombs were dropped. It was felt that this was to create panic among the British people and divert British aircraft from military work in France. In consequence there was anti-German rioting in the East End of London.

A mathematician worked out the chance of escape if fifty Zeppelins raided. If they concentrated on the Metropolitan area the chance of escape would be about 70,000 to 1. If the attack was on the centre of London, this would fall to 1,500 to 1. In Manchester the figure was calculated to be 1,300 to 1. It was felt unlikely that the number of Zeppelins in any raid would exceed fifty. Indeed, at the time this calculation occurred there had been no raids but this would soon change.

The British government ensured that measures were taken should Zeppelins attack the mainland. Though some provisions of the Defence of the Realm Act may seem strange, they served a purpose. Flying a kite or lighting a bonfire could attract Zeppelins and were therefore banned. Locally, Walsall police warned of the remote probability of an aircraft raid ever reaching the town. A hooter or siren would sound at various locations but only by order of the police. All those hearing the hooter must immediately take cover. Occupants of buildings were responsible for ensuring no light from inside was visible externally.

A further order was issued to all firms holding government contracts to ensure that they screened all visible outside lights between sunset and sunrise. If this was impossible they should be able to extinguish visible lights with fifteen minutes' notice. However, the reduction in light from these measures led to potential danger to drivers of vehicles. Councils passed a resolution enforcing the requirement to have rear-facing lights on all vehicles; this was necessary to protect tram operators and drivers of other vehicles.

The Dudley Company of Volunteers was detailed to watch the skies to warn of enemy air attacks. Their signal was three rifle shots (presumably at the Zeppelin), and posters were displayed to reassure the public.

The night of Monday, 31 January 1916 saw the largest aerial raid since the start of the war. It was described as 'of no military value to the enemy: simply murder.' There were two raids: one began at around 7.45pm and the second just before 1am on Tuesday morning. It was thought that six or seven Zeppelins took part, between them dropping over 800 bombs. In fact, nine Zeppelins of the *Kaiserliche Marine* (Imperial German Navy) set out from bases on the north-west coast of Germany. Liverpool was their main target but they failed to hit it.

The first attack at about 8pm involved two airships. At 7.45pm the Zeppelins passed over Wolverhampton and at 7.55pm hovered over Netherton at a height of about 13,000 feet. They then passed over Dudley and reached Tipton at 8pm. The pilot of one airship, Lieutenant Commander Max Dietrich, was hopelessly lost and wasn't even aware he was over the Black Country.

Tipton was the first town attacked. Three bombs fell on Waterloo Street and Union Street, then three incendiaries fell on Bloomfield Street and Barnfield Street, killing thirteen people in two houses. A police sergeant heard the explosion and went to the scene where he found several bodies in the roadway and rescued others from wrecked buildings. There was a huge crater in the road and a gas main had ruptured. A total of fifteen people died in Tipton.

The first bomb to land at Walsall was on Wednesbury Road Congregational Church. There was a preparation class working in the parlour. The teacher, Miss Palmer, saw a small piece of ceiling fall from the roof, then a blinding flash followed by a terrific explosion. The bomb struck the centre of the church roof but no one inside was killed or seriously injured. Thomas Merrylees, aged 28, was not so lucky: he was killed by flying debris from the church.

Other bombs fell on Walsall, including one in the grounds of the General Hospital. Another hit Elijah Jeffries Saddlery Works and the last landed in the town centre on Bradford Place, speculation being that it was aimed at the railway station. It was this bomb that seriously injured Mrs Mary Julia Slater, Mayoress of Walsall, in her chest and abdomen. She was travelling by tram to attend a public meeting when the bomb landed. She died from shock and septicaemia on 20 February. The Walsall Cenotaph now marks the spot where this bomb landed.

There was a praiseworthy spirit of calmness during the worst moments; unexploded devices were found and removed quickly to places of safety. The worst single loss of life was to the Morris family of Union Street, Tipton, comprising an elderly couple, a married daughter, her husband and their two children aged 8 and 11, all in one room of their house and killed by the blast from a single bomb. An incendiary device landed on the roof of a theatre full of people; the audience rose to their feet but the leading actor and manager called for people to be calm and started singing the National Anthem. Everyone then waited in the dark for the danger to pass.

At about 8.10pm sweethearts Maud and William Fellows were killed near the Wolverhampton Union Canal; there is a plaque on the wall of the old pumping station at Bradley marking their death. They heard something like 'thunder and lightning' and took shelter by the wall of the pumping station. William was killed outright and Maud was taken to Wolverhampton General Hospital but died from septicaemia twelve days later. At the inquest into Maud's death the jury held the opinion that the Kaiser and Crown Prince were guilty of murder as accessories before the fact.

Tom Cope was an eye-witness to the raid on Bradley. He was in the parish room at St Martin's with the rest of the choir, waiting to start rehearsals for a concert at his school the next day. Miss Maud Hughes was standing by the piano ready to run through her solo when there was a terrific bang and the windows in the parish room shattered. Miss Hughes 'had fallen in a faint.' The youngsters dashed outside to see what had happened.

Tom said: 'Then I saw the Zeppelin – a huge, silent cigar-shape.' He then went home but realized his parents were out at the theatre in Wolverhampton, so he went to his grandparents. At the time of the raid his grandfather had heard a large knock at the door but when he answered there was no one there and he assumed it was a practical joke. The next morning a piece of shrapnel was found near the door and such evidence had to be handed to the police. That same morning Tom and his friends went to the canal-side where Maud and William Fellows had been killed, near Pothouse Bridge and the old pumping station, to see the crater made by the bomb. Once the Zeppelins had passed over Walsall they headed towards Burton and Derby. This ended the first of two raids that night.

At about 12.30am the Zeppelin engines were heard again over Walsall. Bombs fell in the Birchills and Pleck areas of the town, seriously damaging buildings; for example, the premises of Mr Barton, a carriage-builder. At Wednesbury there was a lucky escape: James Russell Tube Works was hit and seriously damaged but its workers were on strike, thereby minimizing casualties. In total thirty-five people died in Bradley, Tipton, Wednesbury and Walsall. Thousands of people saw the raid but little was recorded contemporaneously about the event. Zeppelin L19 was shot down on the way home from the raid by rifle fire from Dutch soldiers.

It was believed that Walsall suffered as badly as it did because of insufficient lighting restrictions. The raid overturned people's perceptions that they were immune to Zeppelin attack, meaning that street lights and other unshaded lights had still been left burning.

The War Office statement said that the raid was hampered by a thick mist and hit targets in a number of counties including Lincolnshire, Derbyshire and Staffordshire. An official telegram from Berlin declared the raid had hit docks, harbours and factories in and around Liverpool and Birkenhead, as well as other industrial works; no mention at all of the Black Country. The official response was that the raiders simply did not know where they were dropping their bombs. Official casualties were 59 dead and 101 wounded, half being women and children. Only two factories, neither of military significance, were damaged; also a church and a brewery as well as a number of houses.

Early newspaper reports were heavily censored and details of names or places went unreported; instead a blanked space replaced any sensitive information. Coroners' inquests were held on all of the dead, with one saying: 'there was a sad lack of provision on the part of some people that those airships were able to get into the very centre of England, and that they began to operate before any warning was given to people there.' This coroner also commented on the importance of war work and that striking was not helping to bring the war to a close.

The aforementioned Tom Cope told of a story that 'went the rounds' at the time; that of a Tipton man who was asked: ''Ow did yer get on last night in the raid?' His purported reply was: 'The missus broke 'er arm dashin' downstairs, but thank god me pijuns (pigeons) am alright.' Clearly the famous Black Country sense of humour was not entirely diminished because of the raid!

Quick to respond to the Zeppelin raids, Maple & Co. advertised a stock of materials for 'anti-zep blinds' available for immediate delivery. Zeppelin insurance was also offered and one policy was free from *John Bull* magazine. First established in London in 1820, the original popular periodical appeared until 1892; other magazines with the same title were then in existence until at least 1957.

John Bull *magazine offered free insurance against Zeppelin damage.*

The aftermath of the raid

After the raid local mayors and district councils requested that all lights be protected and churches agreed to hold evening services earlier than usual so that they finished before lighting was necessary. Street lamps were shaded and projecting kerbs at important corners were removed. While inconvenient, these measures were welcomed by the people. Cars with big headlights were seen as a problem and the police were asked how they could be dealt with. Action in case of further raids was discussed and a meeting took place involving medical and emergency service personnel. Bedclothing was stockpiled and first-aid provision organized. Aliens were discussed, although according to Dudley police only three remained there.

In Wednesbury similar discussions took place and problems such as light from furnaces and the sounding of bull horns were discussed. It was agreed a committee was needed to deal with such issues and the War Office and Home Office were lobbied about air-raid precautions. A police notice, encouraged by the Home Secretary, urged people to make as little use as possible of the telephone during future air-raids. It warned against 'inconsiderate and unnecessary use of the telephone by private subscribers', which had hampered operations during the recent raids. If this warning was not heeded, the Postmaster General would consider curtailing facilities to private subscribers during periods of emergency.

On 8 February 1916 Lighting Orders came into force: all lamps, flares and fixed lights had to be extinguished, except those public lamps deemed necessary by the police. Any lights not extinguished needed to be reduced to a minimum and shaded to render them invisible from above. Similar measures were ordered in houses, hotels and flats to prevent anything other than a dull, subdued light to be seen from outside. Measures in factories and workshops were to reduce light without curtailing war work. Transport also had regulations and in the case of sudden emergency all instructions given by police, military and naval authorities must immediately be obeyed. As a result the Opera House at Dudley reduced shows to one per night instead of two. The first show affected was *Dare-Devil Dorothy*, a musical comedy review (or 'revusical').

The worry was of future raids. There was criticism of a Lighting Order issued by the Dudley chief constable. It was worded so as to be almost incomprehensible, even to a lawyer. A simple, lucid message was needed. Agreement on a warning signal was a real problem and at Tipton Gasworks the installation of a large hooter was agreed, to warn locals of hostile aircraft. Advice given to the public was that raids after 2.30am were unlikely. This was issued because since the January raid many people were frightened to go upstairs to sleep.

In April the question of how to warn the population of an impending raid was still being debated and it became clear that no one was able

Dudley Opera House (date unknown).

to find a solution that suited the whole region. The hooter was thought to be the answer in Dudley but not in nearby Smethwick. It had been discussed in Parliament and it was said that: 'the people have been stirred up to a high pitch of indignation.' The debate raged: were mobile anti-aircraft guns an option; what about the effect of Lighting Orders; could the telephone be the answer to warn people? The unasked question was about further raids, rendering all other arguments inconsequential! Chief Superintendent Speke of Dudley police announced in the newspaper that no steam whistles, bulls or hooters could be sounded for ordinary purposes between 6pm and 5.30am. Dudley had solved its air-raid warning problem. Wednesbury were still discussing their plans on the subject.

However, the lighting and hooter debate raged around local newspapers. The problem was lack of consensus. One suggestion was for the chief constables of Staffordshire and Worcestershire to meet and make a decision that would be binding on all towns. A spin on this was to invite all mayors of the Black Country to join in the debate. The problem was seen as a major one and the public was told to expect even greater air-raids than the one in January. One imponderable was the possible effect of sounding any form of warning, as it was felt an alert might bring people out of their homes and into greater danger.

By December a new way was found to destroy Zeppelins: it would be fitted to an aeroplane and was said to be certain to bring down the German menace. Tests had been conducted very successfully but the report did not disclose details of the new weapon. Traditional ammunition was not very effective against the Zeppelin but experiments in bullet technology led to incendiary bullets being designed in combination with explosive and tracer rounds. The first Zeppelin shot down in Britain was SL11 on the night of 2–3 September 1916 near Cuffley, London, by Lieutenant William Leefe Robinson. The Zeppelin crew were all killed and Leefe Robinson received a Victoria Cross for his actions.

On 17 June 1917 Gotha bombers attacked London causing 158 fatalities with 425 wounded; the worst British civilian casualties of the war. This incident reignited the issue in local newspapers, both generally and specifically, by reporting on council debates. These reports heightened local fears in the Black Country that there could be a repeat of the carnage caused on the night of 31 January 1916.

Zeppelin raids continued over England with eastern counties bearing the brunt of the attacks and London was also hit. The only casualties reported at the time were the deaths of a cow and a number of pigeons. However, the much later account of that raid reported twenty-seven people killed and a further fifty-three wounded. Some good news was that the allies now had anti-aircraft weapons, which had shot down a Zeppelin over France.

In January 1918 daylight raids by German Gotha bombers again raised fears in the Black Country. Questions were raised at Walsall Council about how to inform the public of such raids, should they occur. The matter was given to the chief constable to deal with. Two years after the infamous first raid and this basic problem had still not been successfully resolved!

CHAPTER 6

1916:
The Realization

Timeline of events

- 1 January: Ministry of Munitions assumes control of the blast furnaces of the Midlands
- 24 January: First Military Service Bill passed by House of Commons
- 27 January: Above Bill becomes Act imposing conscription on all single men aged 18 to 41 in Britain
- 31 January: Airship raid on England, including Black Country, resulting in 183 casualties countrywide
- 16 February: War Office takes over anti-aircraft defence of London and becomes responsible for general anti-aircraft defence
- 21 February: Battle of Verdun begins (ends 31 August)
- 10 May: Agreement signed at Berlin on employment of British and German prisoners of war
- 21 May: German attack on Vimy Ridge
- 8 June: Second Compulsory Service Act comes into operation in Britain
- 1 July: Battle of the Somme begins (ends 18 November)
- 28 November: First German daylight raid on London (by single aeroplane)
- 7 December: Lloyd George succeeds Asquith as British prime minister

- 11 December: Lloyd George's Coalition Ministry formed
- 22 December: Ministry of Food and Ministry of Pensions formed in Britain
- 29 December: Rasputin murdered in Petrograd

Europe was now an immense battlefield with no apparent end in sight. Both sides were well-matched and the tactics used at the front were bound to deliver massive casualties, death and serious injury, impacting on almost every family in the Black Country. Our region was drawn closer to the front on 31 January when Zeppelin airships, intending to bomb the north-west, instead created a swathe of horror across the Black Country, causing many deaths, injuries and much damage.

Battle of the Somme 1916
The Battle of the Somme took place between 1 July and 18 November 1916. It was controversial because of the tactics employed and was significant as tanks were used for the first time. On the first day of fighting the British lost more than 19,000 men including 60 per cent of all officers involved. Total casualties during the battle amounted to 420,000 and this perhaps comprised the worst loss of life during the whole First World War period.

It was reported that the Black Country was prospering because of the war, with many works operating night and day. Examples included extensions being made to the Britannia Works of the Cable Accessories Company and to the Vono Works in Tipton Road, Tividale.

Recruitment problems, as described in the last chapter, resulted in conscription and this situation will be described in more detail. As New Year dawned, the response to the call for men to enlist reached 3,000,000; the greatest voluntary army in world history. Under Lord Derby's scheme men who were 'starred' (i.e. essential war workers) were exempt from service. This system was not ideal, although the concept seemed sound as it was as important to provide equipment for the armed forces as it was to send men to the front. However, priorities regarding what was considered essential war work adapted as needs changed and the demand for men at the front increased.

Prime Minister Herbert Asquith introduced a bill for compulsory attestation in early January 1916. Single men, or widowers without children, of military age who had no grounds or excuse for exemption were treated as though they had attested for enlistment. Men entitled to exemption were those engaged on 'necessary national work', single men who were the 'stay and support' of their relatives, those suffering ill-health or infirmity and conscientious objectors to the undertaking of combatant service. Initially some trades thought they were exempt from joining up and these included some Walsall leather-makers who were making much of the equipment for the cavalry and horse transport. Leather workers were actually encouraged to sign up to fill gaps left by those who had died, according to the *Walsall Observer*. One of the measures the Compulsion Bill proposed was a special reserve of 'soldier workers' who could be moved wherever they were needed around the country until required as soldiers.

The Braggart: 'It was I who opened fire on Rheims.'

The Derby Scheme ran in tandem with Asquith's Bill; Derby grouped all men who attested into forty-six groups. The first twenty-three comprised unmarried men and these were called up first, then married men's groups followed. Groups two to five were called up in the last two weeks of January 1916 and groups six to thirteen in February. The last single groups, other than 18-year-olds, were called up in March. This last batch was called up in parallel with the first men summoned under conscription by the Military Service Act, attestation under the Derby Scheme having ceased on 1 March 1916. Recruits were not necessarily posted to local regiments and from this time onwards it was not wise for a recruit to assume a man would go into his local regiment. Group Scheme recruits rarely had a say in where they were assigned.

There were some humorous moments reported when men arrived to attest. For example, one was asked if his wife was a widow or spinster when they married and he replied: 'No, a bolt-screwer.'

Another, when asked which regiment he would like to join, replied 'the Royal Flying Corpse'. There were some underhand means used to persuade men, even underage boys, to sign up. NCOs were paid by results and almost inevitably this led to some 'sharp practices'. There is anecdotal evidence of local Volunteer Corps members selecting a popular young man who was sent out to recruit his friends, while being held back himself from being recruited in order to carry out this work.

One aspect of the Derby Scheme was the introduction of local tribunals where men who had attested could appeal for a delay in being sent into the forces. Tribunals were set up around the Black Country and were a feature of all weekly newspapers, although no names of men who made such applications were published. Dudley Council was one that appointed a tribunal for this purpose and ten men formed the tribunal.

Around the Black Country tribunals heard cases of men who had attested and were then called up. Many applicants for exemption were seeking such because of personal or employment reasons. In many cases applications were made by their employer. The House of Lords debated the tribunals and Lord Sandhurst said: 'The War Office agreed to abide by the decisions of these Tribunals, subject to the right of appeal to a central body, but this was merely an administrative arrangement without legal sanction.' Having attested, men became soldiers, no matter what the local tribunal decided and the War Office agreed to abide by the decision of the tribunal. This distinguished the local tribunal as being separate from those set up under the Military Service Act, which decided if a man should be a soldier or remain a civilian. Local tribunal members did not seem to realize the significance of this nuance. Some tribunals were harsher than others. Tipton was seen as the strictest with more direct refusals than any other part of the Black Country but Dudley also vied for this title. Furthermore, Black Country tribunals were seen as being stricter than those in any other part of the country.

An interesting refusal was for a 'cook and carver': this was pleaded on the grounds that a woman could not lift heavy joints or pans and it was work for a man. A 31-year-old from West Bromwich tried to claim exemption from military service because of corns. His case was adjourned for a month for a further medical examination.

Conscientious objectors

These were people who did not want to fight in the war: they were known as 'conscies' or simply 'COs'. Several reasons were identified for being a CO: pacifists who were generally against war; political objectors, who did not consider Germany to be their enemy; religious objectors who believed that war and fighting were against their religion. The latter included Quakers and Jehovah's Witnesses. Finally there were those who claimed the status for multiple reasons. Some were keen to help the war effort but not to fight. Some worked in munitions factories and others went to the front as stretcher-bearers and in other non-combatant roles. The War Office was reportedly seriously concerned about the freedom given by local tribunals on exempting or considerably delaying enlistment of conscientious objectors. It was noted that this approach was not the case in the Black Country.

One Tipton CO brought a friend to represent him. He said the State had no right to violate his religious convictions, which he had held for a number of years. He was placed in the non-combatant service and told by Councillor Doughty that 'It will make a man of you.' Another Tipton man asked to be exempted because he was a follower of Christ, who was an Ambassador of Peace. He was told: 'Your soul belongs to God, and the body belongs to your King and Country. As far as I am concerned we shall deliver the goods.' He was given a two-month extension on domestic grounds.

Four Christadelphians appeared as conscientious objectors after three weeks' exemption to allow them to find national war work. They had found no work and refused to volunteer to work in France. They claimed their grounds amounted to a special exemption but the tribunal claimed no knowledge of this. Mr Doughty of the tribunal said: 'I should sign an order that would place them in the forefront, and then they might stop a bullet from hitting a better man.' The matter was left in the hands of the military authorities regarding what should be done about the men; an example of the confusion between 'Derby' tribunals and Military Service Act decisions.

Aliens and spies

Across the region police collated the names of all Germans resident in the area and whether they were properly supervised. The police acted in accordance with government regulations regarding identification, registration and staying within 5 miles of the town unless they had a warrant allowing them to go outside that area. Aliens were kept under observation, mainly by Specials, and I could find no reports of attempts to evade regulations.

At Pensnett on Wednesday, 27 January 1916 there was sensational news that two German spies were operating in the village. At 1pm one of the two men was seen loitering on Commonside. A crowd quickly gathered, one estimate being that up to 1,000 women and children had gathered in the area of Bromley Lane and Commonside. However, this was a false alarm! The 'spy' was wearing an Inverness coat but was of singular appearance as he was not wearing his 'nether garments' and looked a sorry spectacle. The crowd had come to see a spy and their disappointment turned to anger. The 'spy' entered a field at the rear of the Fish Inn and licensee Mr Aston took it upon himself to single-handedly capture the man, armed only with a stick. Aston waved the crowd back and, keeping a sharp lookout for weapons, approached the man. Our erstwhile spy turned out to be docile and only wanted to escape the crowd. PC Gripton arrived on the scene and apprehended the man who was taken to Brierley Hill Police Station. It was found that he was a harmless Irishman and Superintendent Johnson ordered him to be removed to the Poor Law Union Workhouse. This would have been the workhouse at Wordsley, Stourbridge, which later became Wordsley Hospital.

Work for women

Dudley was one town that set up courses for women in early 1916 so they could take up clerk posts. In May the Technical School at Dudley advertised a further course aimed at training ladies to type; this was a ten-week course and ran for five nights a week for ten weeks at three hours per night and the cost was 25 shillings per student.

Walsall explored offering similar courses but discovered that only a dozen firms were in need of women clerks; little justification for the courses. There was plenty of work to be had around the region, with one advert in January reading: 'Girls wanted age 11–16 for leather work and light press work, Mason, 45 Newhall Hill (Birmingham).' Some restrictions on this type of advert were imposed by the government. Adverts from firms in engineering, shipbuilding, production of arms and ammunition, explosives or substances required to make explosives had to carry the message: 'No person more than 10 miles away or already engaged on war business (may apply).'

The training of munitions workers was paramount and resources were provided by both the industry and science departments to assist. Staff and machinery were provided for the training and technical adaptations were made to existing machines, enabling mass-production of munitions. In the Black Country classes were held in Wednesbury, Willenhall and West Bromwich and most courses were open to both sexes. Production of parts to make new machines to meet the demands of the war was a priority and these machines were built to a very high specification.

The Black Country furnished 600 women from June to September for fruit-picking and other work in Worcestershire and Staffordshire counties. There was already a local tradition of this type of seasonal work such as hop-picking in Worcestershire and Herefordshire, a popular summer holiday break for families in the Black Country. What differed was that the organization of the workforce was done by local councils.

By the middle of the war some workers at West Bromwich firm George Salter's were 'badged' by as many as four government

George Salter's Spon Lane Foundry, 1898.

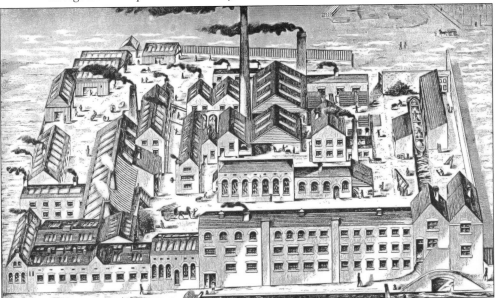

departments. The number of women working for the company had increased massively; day and night shifts were worked and a 'volunteer' shift of Sunday workers was inaugurated. Women from various occupations gave up their Sunday leisure so that factory hands could have an occasional day off.

Aftermath of the Zeppelin raids

While the Zeppelin raid of 31 January 1916 is covered in an earlier chapter, there were ramifications for one Cradley Heath shopkeeper. Old Hill Police Court heard the case of six young people aged between 14 and 18 who smashed the windows of a shop owned by Harry Harris (or Hirsh Demboski) on 2 February 1916. The value of the windows was £20 and all the defendants pleaded guilty. It was believed by some in Cradley Heath, possibly fuelled by the recent Zeppelin raids, that Harris was German. Inspector Myatt and some of his men saw the crowd gather at the shop and suggested that Harris close for the day. Harris was a naturalized British citizen but born in Russia; he and his wife ran two shops in the town.

The following day the shop windows were smashed by the defendants. Mrs Miriam Harris gave evidence at the hearing and when asked if she said anything sympathetic about Germans, she replied that she had brothers in Russia fighting against the Germans and cousins fighting with the British against the Germans, so why would she?

While the Zeppelin raid shocked the Black Country and was the catalyst for much change, life went on. *Dare-Devil Dorothy* paid a welcome visit to Dudley Opera House. Owing to the dark streets, due to lighting restrictions, she only performed once nightly instead of twice but two matinees were scheduled during her run to accommodate more people. The title role was played by Miss Ida Conroy, apparently known throughout the world for her 'sprightliness'.

In early March the first prosecutions for not shading inside lights were reported. There were cases in Langley, Oldbury and Warley. Twelve defendants appeared at Oldbury Police Court and most defendants were fined 10s. Similar cases were reported across the Black Country, with one shopkeeper in Wolverhampton Street, Dudley being fined 20s for a serious breach. Newspapers began printing the times of the rising and setting of the sun. Due to lighting restrictions, gas consumption decreased which helped to reduce supply problems.

Ida Conroy.

In April an interesting article was published from the front detailing a football tournament. The Fanshawe Cup, named after General Edward Arthur Fanshawe, the corps commander, reached its final on 23 March 1916. It was played 'somewhere in France' and local interest was high as the 1st Bucks Battalion played a team from the 7th Battalion Worcestershire Regiment. Some 2,500 soldiers lined the touchline, just behind the firing line, and the divisional band played to while away the time before kick-off. Traditional crowd accompaniments such as tin cans, clappers and mouth organs were 'played', making it a typical cup final crowd. Dudley was very well represented in the team, with five players coming from the town. A lone Halesowen player added to the Black Country contingent. The Worcesters immediately applied pressure on their opponents and Doctor Jeffrey from Kidderminster soon scored the first goal. The score at half time was 1–0 to the Worcesters. The crowd grew to 3,000 as the second half began and the Bucks attacked in strength but were thwarted in every attack. Doctor Jeffrey scored a fine second goal fifteen minutes from time, which sealed the game for our lads.

A shortage of petrol became a reality as the war progressed. Motoring journalists said that owners of motor cars had been economizing since the start of the war but elsewhere there was great waste. Army lorry engines were regularly left running while the vehicles were loaded or unloaded and the same lorries were used for short errands that could easily be done by bicycle. Petrol was said to be used by the army for cleaning, not only of engines but also the outside of the lorry. Many companies carrying out war work were also supplied with much more petrol than they required, with petrol companies negotiating deals directly with manufacturing companies rather than using the national delivery systems.

October saw a fresh series of charity appeals and events. On Wednesday, 18 October 1916 a concert was held on behalf of the British society for the relief of wounded Belgian soldiers. There was also a call for warm items of hand-knitted clothing for soldiers: mittens, mufflers, helmets, gloves, cardigans and socks. Concerns were raised about an entertainment tax that had been introduced: this was 2d in the shilling and the pastor of Upper Gornal Congregational Church criticized application of the tax to purely charitable events as it diminished the 'profits' of the effort.

In mid-November a patriotic football match was held in Dudley, involving teams from both Wolves and Albion. The match benefited the Tipton Soldiers and Sailors Comforts Fund. Some 5,000 people attended, most of whom paid 1d a time for small bows in aid of the fund. Wednesbury Victoria Cross hero Sergeant James Davies kicked off the match. He had recently been discharged from the army and was much celebrated in local newspapers as one of our greatest heroes. Jesse Pennington was one famous local player involved. The final score was 1–0 to Wolves; the two footballs used in the game were auctioned and raised almost £9 for the charity.

In December the Dudley Guest Hospital Christmas Fund publicized its regular Christmas appeal. Hospital expenses had been unusually heavy as 1916 had seen the opening of a brand-new surgical outpatients and Eye Department. It had been a difficult year with increased workload, higher prices and reduced income; 1,444 patients had been treated, which was a record for the hospital. The number attending the outpatients department was 13,200 and the Eye Department also showed increased attendance. The hospital's X-ray machine broke down because of heavy usage and had not been replaced by the end of the year, so patients needing X-rays were sent to Birmingham. The Ladies Linen League saved money by providing many necessary articles for the wards. The total deficit for the year was £1,388. Finally, a warning of staff shortages was given due to doctors and

Sergeant James Davies VC of Tipton. (Tipton Library)

One of two plaques commemorating the fallen of Tipton, on permanent display in Tipton Library.

senior nurses volunteering to work in larger war hospitals or at the front. Similar financial problems beset Walsall Manor hospital.

Christmas 1916 must have been received with muted feelings for Black Country residents. The Battle of the Somme had concluded on 18 November and the carnage of that campaign led to huge numbers of casualties. Churchill described the campaign 'from beginning to end a welter of slaughter.' Monthly British casualty figures for the campaign are telling. In July nearly 200,000 men died in the first month of the campaign. Then an average of 76,000 British soldiers died each month for the following four months. Following the Somme campaign, December saw only 13,803 men die, a comparatively low number! The war in France remained very bitter and a truce for the soldiers was seen as unlikely but there were glimpses of humanity: Canadian and German troops at Vimy Ridge reached out to each other in friendship and to trade gifts.

In the Black Country this would be another 'stay-at-home' Christmas for many. The weather was again abysmal, the worst snowfall since the 1880s was recorded, trams ran late and there were many cancellations. There was a call for greater economy at home; food supplies were a cause for concern due to German naval action which affected both price and supply of essentials such as meat and bread. Hotels were very quiet; regulations normally dictated that only two courses could be served at mealtimes but this was relaxed for Christmas Day and three courses were allowed. Liquor control regulations were again relaxed so that people had more opportunity to purchase supplies in the run-up to the holiday.

Entertainment at the newly-extended Criterion Cinema in Dudley over Christmas was extensive. Owner Sidney Bray arranged a non-stop show from 2.30pm to 10.30pm on Christmas Eve. Then on Boxing Day entertainment started at 11am with 'first class pictures' and from 2.30pm a continuous run of films.

On Boxing Day another patriotic football match took place, with two teams from Harper, Sons & Bean playing at Dudley County Ground. The game was hard-fought but the final 5–0 score told a different story. A large number of tickets were sold and the traditional auction for the match ball helped to swell funds for the Dudley Patriotic Committee.

Good news reported on 30 December was that Private Frank Hunt

The Criterion Cinema, Dudley.

was at home on leave for a month, after having served continuously since the beginning of the war. He reported a number of scrapes and near misses, especially while digging advance trenches but he had not been injured. He had met HRH The Prince of Wales numerous times and was at the front to see the first batch of tanks arrive and go into action. Frank had married just fourteen days before going to the front. This was a classic example of propaganda designed to balance the horrific stories and casualty figures.

The second great climax, as described by Churchill, came at the start of 1917. Three events marked the beginning of the year: the German declaration of unlimited U-boat activities; the intervention of the United States, leading to their entry into the war; and the Russian Revolution …

A 1914 4HP Sunbeam 600cc motorcycle made in Wolverhampton during the First World War, only supplied to the French military. (Black Country Living Museum)

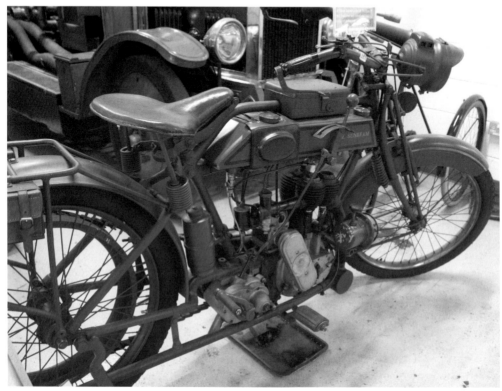

CHAPTER 7

1917:
Seeing it Through

Timeline of events

- 3 February: United States severs diplomatic relations with Germany
- 12 March: Russian Revolution begins
- 6 April: United States declares war on Germany
- 7 May: First night air-raid on London; single aeroplane by moonlight
- 19 May: US government announces decision to send a division of the US army to France at once
- 7 June: Battle of Messines (1917) begins allied offensive in Flanders
- 25 June: First contingent of US troops arrives in France
- 28 July: Tank Corps formed in British army
- 20 September: Battle of Menin Road Ridge (Ypres) begins
- 12 October: First Battle of Passchendaele (Ypres)
- 6 November: Passchendaele captured by British (Canadian) forces
- 20 November: Battle of Cambrai begins
- 7 December: United States declares war on Austria-Hungary

After almost three years of war the United States finally declared war on Germany. The Germans had declared unrestricted submarine warfare against Britain. They realized this would eventually bring America into the conflict but the British naval blockade was having a serious impact on Germany. Germany hoped to force Britain to sue for peace before America declared war but that was not the case. Britain did suffer heavy losses, on average over 500,000 tons of shipping per month. In August Britain adopted a convoy system, which vastly reduced the effectiveness of this German strategy by protecting merchant ships with warships.

Another weapon deployed against the U-boats was the Q-ship or mystery (decoy) ship. One Walsall man, Charles George Bonner, received a Victoria Cross for his part on one of these ships, the *Dunraven*, in August 1917. Bonner's citation read: 'For conspicuous gallantry and consummate skill and coolness in action with an enemy submarine.' No news was reported of the award until November to preserve the surprise element of the Q-ships, which were heavily armed but disguised as merchant ships, designed to lure U-boats to the surface to engage the victim with their gun instead of using their limited torpedo supply. In 1915 and 1916 the Germans lost eleven U-boats

Victoria Cross.

due to this ruse; eventually they were forced to stay well clear of merchant ships and only attack them with torpedoes.

At home, conditions for people living in the Black Country were continually worsening. Bread rationing was introduced in February and newspaper prices increased because of the rising price of paper, a shortage of materials and higher wages. Canny housewives stored old newspapers to sell to fishmongers. Why not? Paper was 9d per pound during this period. It was reported that it took a sovereign (which had a nominal value of £1 sterling) to pay for what had cost 12 shillings before the war. The 30s weekly allowance to a war wife with four children was becoming inadequate.

In January a Wordsley furnace man, Joseph Hancox, was charged with supplying beer to sick soldiers. He bought six bottles of Guinness stout from the Bear Inn at Wordsley to take out. Benjamin Cotton saw two wounded soldiers (distinguishable by their blue uniform trousers) talking to Hancox, who then went into the public house and returned, giving the men the beer. Hancox claimed he didn't know he was doing anything wrong. He had failed to read notices that this action was an offence because he had been away serving in the navy. He was fined £3 and ordered to pay 2s and 6d to each of the two witnesses (Benjamin Cotton and Florence Stantiall, licensee of The Bear.

Desertion was common and this was regularly reported in local newspapers. One Amblecote mother, Lizzie Bastock, was charged with harbouring her soldier son, Albert Weychan, a military deserter. He had been on the run since March 1916. Around Christmas 1916 Police Sergeant Beddowes went to the Bastock house and took the precaution of posting an officer at the rear. Lizzie said her son was not in the house. Weychan, spooked by the sergeant, ran out through the kitchen door and, after a pursuit in the dark, he escaped. His mother was fined £2 or twenty-one days in prison for harbouring a deserting soldier.

On 24 January 1917 the persistent Sergeant Beddowes again visited the family address. This time he searched the upstairs rooms and found a ladder against a lean-to roof. On further investigation Weychan was found in the cellar of a vacant shop next door. When he appeared at Brierley Hill Magistrates Weychan said he was a conscientious objector who hadn't had a fair hearing at his tribunal application. He also said the chairman of his appeal tribunal told him he had no conscience! He was fined 40 shillings by the court and handed over to the military authorities.

In late January the chief constable of Staffordshire called for all married police constables under 25 and single constables under 30 to submit to medical examination with a view to entering the army. Police pay in Staffordshire was also under scrutiny and officers were in a state of revolt. The average married constable's pay was no longer a living wage and had fallen below the poverty line. It would take until October 1918 for a new pay structure for all police officers to be adopted. This included basic pay and increments depending on service in rank. Good conduct also played a part in the incremental pay awards. A Police Representative Board was proposed to deal with matters of conditions of service and welfare.

In February it was the miners who came under the spotlight for further recruitment into the army. Colliery courts were held to hear cases generated by a travelling medical board, examining men of military age who had entered the industry after August 1915. A large number of men were released for military service by this process. This action was possible because there had been a reduction in the demand for coal, both at home and for export. Some trades were exempted, including winding-engine men and wagon- and tub-makers. The local miners' association passed a resolution strongly protesting against possible employment of women in or around mines.

War loans were being taken out by firms across the Black Country; in addition local urban and rural district councils were loaning money to the war effort. The rate paid in interest was 5 per cent. Employees were encouraged to 'buy' smaller loans from their employer, with interest to be paid weekly.

Wounded soldiers in the Military Hospital at Wordsley were taught various forms of handiwork as a result of an initiative of the committee of the lady mayoress (of Birmingham). The work included rug- and basket-making and knitting. Patients were able to keep the work they produced upon payment for materials used and any surplus was sold at the committee's shop in Ethel Street, Birmingham. The hospital was converted from Wordsley Infirmary in the summer of 1915 and had

Richardson Hall, Wordsley, as it appears today.

510 beds. It was the Stourbridge annexe of the
Southern General Hospital, which included
buildings at the University of Birmingham,
the old Poor Law infirmary on Dudley Road
and a number of further annexes in
Birmingham, including Selly Park.

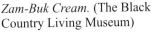

By March casualty numbers were again
rising in all hospitals in the Black Country.
Wordsley Hospital was one location that
needed to expand. Nearby Richardson Hall,
Wordsley was turned into a sleeping-place for
sixty wounded soldiers. Beds and mattresses
were brought in, ventilators knocked out –
leaving many holes in the walls – and pictures

Zam-Buk Cream. (The Black
Country Living Museum)

were taken down. The hall had previously been used for drill by local
Special Constables and volunteers. It was also used for church services
as it was difficult to effectively black-out the church.

One regular feature of newspapers was adverts for various remedies
for a wide variety of medical conditions. One
such product made sweeping claims to be
able to cure many ailments: Zam-Buk was
'The Great Herbal Balm' and could cure
bruises, scratches, ulcers, pimples, piles,
chilblains and much more. It also claimed to
have healed men so they became fit enough
to join up. Zam-Buk is still sold today but is
no longer making such extravagant claims. It
is mainly sold online and users enthuse about
its qualities.

The employment of women had brought
about major social change in Britain. In parts
of the Black Country the employment of
women bank clerks was questioned. Some
customers objected to being served by a 'girl'
clerk, although ironically it seems many of
these objectors were women customers!
People were advised not to entertain such
prejudice; banks had said that women were

Zam-Buk advert.

equal to male clerks in terms of performance and that they were willing and accurate when carrying out their duties.

There was also criticism of the Midland Tramway Company for their decision to employ women tram drivers on some Black Country routes. It was said that this was dangerous to the public, pedestrians and vehicular traffic. The local Trades Council wrote to the Board of Trade, Minister of Munitions and the Tramway Company to voice their concerns.

In March newspaper prices again rose due to a shortage of materials. The *County Express* newspaper started a campaign where readers were urged to share their papers with others. If everyone shared their newspaper with one neighbour, then one ton of paper could be saved each issue.

The Midlands Iron and Steel Trades Red Cross Fund donated six new ambulances, which were graciously accepted by King George V. The generosity of the donation was praised by His Majesty. The ambulances were to be distributed throughout the army.

Allotments and home-growing had become a necessity to avoid malnutrition or even starvation. Stourbridge residents were informed that they could contact the headmaster of Stourbridge Grammar School if they needed help with digging, planting and seeding their garden. Boys from the school were available during April to carry out this work.

Local tribunals were used to hearing cases of men who were eligible for military service and, as previously mentioned, our tribunals were among the harshest in the country with a very high refusal rate. One case that they allowed was that of two night-soil workers. The local authority gave evidence that they could not find anyone else to do the men's jobs. Their representative began to tell the tribunal of the horrid state of affairs if the men were required for military service. The Chair stopped him, saying: 'We know that, we do not want to advertise it.' Exemption until June 1917 was granted. I have no doubt that at the next hearing the exemption would have been extended further.

In May in Sedgley 4 acres of land were taken over under the Cultivation of Land Order. There was great demand for the allotments this land provided and over 300 applications were received. In June at Tipton almost all allotment space had been taken. Local newspapers also regularly published columns which gave cultivation advice. One

Stourbridge Grammar School in the early twentieth century.

regular correspondent was 'Rambler' in the *Tipton Herald*, whose growing advice in June was to plant leeks when space became available. The leek was a favourite with the ancient Egyptian Pharaohs, later adopted by the Israelites and then the 'fiery' Celts. It could be grown in all types of soil, 'road dirt' suited them best and it was hailed as having 'high dietetic value'. However, an advert, a warning, forecast a shortage of all kinds of seeds for 1918 and advised people only to buy the quantity they required.

The Metropolitan Carriage, Wagon and Finance Company reported increased growth in business at its 15th annual meeting in July. Their success was tinged with regret that the growth was due to supplying increased amounts of war material: 'For more than two and a half years we have been practically divorced from our ordinary trade … our works have been converted into an arsenal … turning out engines of war and equipment of all kinds.' We will see later how crucial the company became, especially in tank-building.

In the summer of 1917 another war was declared against a natural enemy: wasps! Due to the wasps annoying horses and cattle and causing damage to crops, the Food Production Department urged that nests should be burned or smoked with paraffin or sulphur if cyanide could not be obtained. In 1915 it had been the humble fly that was under attack; now the 'wasp front' was opened!

The summer saw the usual round of charity events take place around the Black Country. The fête at Dudley Priory was a great success and plenty of money was raised. 'Love', the Red Cross donkey, alone raised hundreds of pounds! Other games included 'Kicking at the Kaiser'. Various items were auctioned, including a row of potatoes planted in front of the Priory which raised £69 16s. The potatoes were still growing and the buyer, Alderman George Bean, having paid over £52 for them, gave them back to be sold again. Another auction immediately followed for the potatoes, raising a further £17. They then remained on the market until fully grown when they would be sold once again to raise yet more funds. Gross takings over the two days were £2,000 and the final total raised was £2,400.

Something infrequently reported on was the rate of suicide among servicemen, despite it becoming more prevalent. In early August 1917 Edward Jones hanged himself in his bedroom on the day he was due to return to barracks. A letter that he left made it clear that the horrors going through his mind were what caused him to take his own life.

Coal shortages and gas supply

While it was still summertime, coal shortages became likely. For some time people had been advised to buy and store coal, because from August the Coal Controller was only allowing the purchase of 5cwt per week, not enough to fuel a six- or seven-room house. In December the feared shortage became a reality. Tipton Council prepared to supply coal at 8½d per cwt to residents requiring it. They could buy no more than 3cwt per week and the coal had to be collected from the council store on Monday, Friday or Saturday.

The gas supply was also becoming stretched. In September, for example, low gas pressure in Dudley was a cause for concern, machinery was affected badly and a call went out to the Gas Company to rectify this problem quickly. The growth in industrial output had raised the demand for gas companies, who were struggling to improve the infrastructure to meet demand. To add to the problems, 10,000 Black Country miners went on strike in the north of the region due to delays by the Coal Controller in granting an expected wage increase.

Gas prices increased again in November, partly due to higher wages. To save gas the county police authorities only allowed about a third of street lamps to be illuminated; this was for safety as well as economy. There were still fears of further Zeppelin and aircraft bomber raids over the region.

Remembering the dead

In late 1916 and also during 1917 a number of war shrines and memorials were planned and built. One of the first was dedicated at Blackheath and a large gathering attended the service. It was attached to the wall of a house in Halesowen Street and held the names of fifty-one men who were serving, five of whom had been killed. The first reported on in February 1917 was at St Michael's in Tividale. It was described as a fitting memorial to the fallen of the parish. A short service was held at the shrine, which was made from stout wood and was erected on the opposite side of Dudley Port to Fisher Street. In July a shrine for the fallen of Woodsetton was unveiled, with a special service being held at St Chad's. This honoured those who had given their lives so far during the war. In August plans were declined by the local authority for a war shrine to be erected on the village green at Kingswinford. This was because the council had no jurisdiction over the green. It was eventually built in an apse on the wall of St Mary's Church. In December a memorial lych-gate opened at Brockmoor, Brierley Hill, in front of a large crowd. This was possible because of contributions made by all classes of people in the area. There was a service and several speeches honouring all who had gone to war. The memorial was erected at the entrance to the parish churchyard, roofed with English oak rafters and covered by the best Welsh slate. There were six commemorative panels inside to hold the names of the fallen.

Brockmoor War Memorial. There are still six panels inside the lych-gate but the Great War panels are no longer visible.

Christmas in the Black Country

Christmas plans were drawn up in November and charity events were again organized locally. The Tipton Christmas Gift Fund wanted to raise money to send a gift to each man serving in the army or navy, as well as to discharged men in receipt of a pension. Also it was intended to entertain children of servicemen and finally to contribute to the Red

Cross Society for relief of POWs. They had already raised £68 to add to the £400 left over from 1916.

One pre-Christmas event took place in early December and entertained 150 wounded and disabled soldiers stationed at Wordsley and Stourbridge hospitals. These included Australian, Canadian and ANZAC soldiers; also present were many local men. A concert and afternoon tea were provided. The deputy mayor thanked the organizers and praised the men who had been wounded in the thick of the fighting. An unusual auction at the end of the evening was for a single slice of bread: it raised 5 shillings, which would start the fund for the next similar event.

Women and work

Women must have felt conflicting pressures by the end of 1917. The main conflict was between women's traditional role as home-maker and mother and the 'new' world of work and the possibility of making careers for themselves. The Archbishop of York talked of a new era for women but stated that the greatest career for them remained that of being the mother of a home, despite 'new temptations which were opened up to them'.

Just before the New Year Bean & Son advertised for 1,000 women from Wolverhampton, Walsall and West Bromwich to work at a newly-built factory in Hurst Lane, Tipton, making fuses. The hours were 8am to 6pm and there were good wages to be earned. The advert promised light, clean work and one of the finest canteens in the Midlands. The factory had been built by German prisoners of war and an iron foundry was also built there.

Three crèches were set up by Dudley Town Council to service women working in munitions factories in Dudley, Netherton and Woodside, three-quarters of the cost being met by the government. A house was rented at each location and a responsible person recruited to supervise each crèche. Alderman Bean also announced he would build a maternity hospital next to Firs House in Kates Hill, for which plans were to be submitted in due course. There now appears no sign of the hospital, although Firs House is a doctor's surgery in a prominent position at the edge of Kates Hill. It has previously also been a chest clinic.

A letter to one newspaper concerned high infant mortality and criticized the fact that more women were going into industry and getting more involved with politics. The writer quoted Lord Rhondda, Minister of Food Control, who had said the lives of 50,000 infants might be lost annually by women 'failing to regard their domestic and maternal duties'.

Tanks and the Black Country

The 29-tonne (28.54-ton) Mark V tank was exclusively built by Metropolitan-Cammell Carriage and Wagon Company, situated in Wednesbury. Design production began at the end of 1917 and into June 1918. Some 400 Mark V tanks were produced, plus 700 of a variant of the Mark V (Mark V*). The main change in the variant was that it was longer and the tracks were extended to help it cross wider trenches, the Germans having recently widened their trenches to protect soldiers from tanks. By Armistice Day 579 Mark V* tanks had been built; the remainder were delivered by Metropolitan-Cammell by March 1919. Two surviving Mark Vs are at Bovington Tank Museum and one is in working order.

First World War Mark IV tank located in Ashford town centre, Kent.

CHAPTER 8

1918:
The Final Blows

Timeline of events

- 21 March: First Battles of the Somme 1918 begin with Battle of St Quentin
- 23 March: Paris first shelled by long-range gun (located 75 miles away)
- 1 April: Royal Flying Corps/Royal Naval Air Services amalgamated and Royal Air Force established
- 10 April: Third Military Service Act passed. Service age limit raised to 50. Conscription extended to Ireland
- 12 April: Last airship raid over England where casualties (twenty-seven) were inflicted
- 18 May: First British retaliatory air-raid on German towns. Cologne bombed by day
- 17 July: RMS *Carpathia*, the ship that had rescued survivors from RMS *Titanic*, sunk by U-boat
- 20 July: German forces retreat across the Marne
- 8 August: Allied Amiens offensive or Second Battles of the Somme 1918 begin
- 12 September: Battles of Hindenburg Line begin series of allied offensives
- 15 September: German government makes definite peace offer to Belgium

- 9 October: Cambrai captured by British forces, bringing battles of Hindenburg Line to a close
- 20 October: Belgian coast completely reoccupied by allied forces
- 2 November: Last British merchant vessels (SS *Surada* and *Murcia*) sunk by submarine in the Mediterranean
- 3 November: Allied governments agree to Germany's proposal for armistice and peace
- 5 November: US President Woodrow Wilson sends final note to German government with allied acceptance of armistice proposals
- 9 November: Revolution breaks out in Berlin; Kaiser abdicates
- 11 November: Armistice concluded between allied and associated powers and Germany. Hostilities on Western Front cease at 11am
- 24 November: British and United States troops reach German frontier
- 4 December: Demobilization of British army begins

The Tank Bank

From January 1918 the 'Tank Bank' was a major national fund-raising campaign by the British government. Six Mark IV tanks toured the country promoting government War Bonds and War Savings Certificates. The tanks were named 'Julian', 'Old Bill', 'Nelson', 'Drake', 'Egbert' and 'Iron Ration'. There was a competitive element for each town: the town or city that raised the most money per capita would win the tank 'Egbert'. This prize eventually went to West Hartlepool. In the Black Country Wolverhampton was visited by 'Old Bill' and many other towns were also visited including Smethwick, Dudley and Stourbridge.

'Julian' visited Walsall between 25 and 30 March 1918 and 'Tanking Hours' were 10am to 8pm outside Walsall Town Hall. Its arrival was announced spectacularly by the dropping of pamphlets from an aeroplane. Each town had a fund-raising target and the amounts raised were reported in the national press to generate a competitive spirit. Towns around Walsall pledged

Advert announcing the arrival of the tank.

'Julian' arriving in Brierley Hill led by a military band, passing the junction of North and South Streets with Church Hill. (Dr Paul Collins collection)

assistance, including Wednesbury, Darlaston, Brownhills and Pelsall. People were asked to save their money for the week.

A week before Tank Week ambitious claims were made that £1 million could be raised. There was plenty of effort in schools and businesses to raise money and people were asked to question themselves: 'Am I reserving all my available cash to Bank at the Tank?' The event coincided with Good Friday and it was not certain if business would be done on that day. The week started with a great public meeting at Townsend Park, Walsall, where people were urged to 'Support the Tank'.

On the tank's arrival in Walsall the town's mayor and mayoress and the mayor of Wednesbury were there to meet it. The overriding message was to invest in the Tank Bank but some saw the opportunity to make money for themselves. Four Birmingham men and another from Leeds were arrested for peddling without a licence. They quickly appeared in court and were sentenced to seven days' imprisonment. One of them said they had been following the tank around the country.

Business throughout the week was brisk and over £576,000 was raised by the start of the last day, with a big push called for to achieve the £1 million target. It was Easter Saturday and there was great hope from the mayor 'not to rest until you have achieved a million'. By the end of the week £832,207 had been raised. Heavy rain on Saturday probably deterred some people from turning out but not everyone was put off as £255,000 was raised on the last day. On leaving Walsall, 'Julian' moved on to Dudley.

The scene in Walsall when 'Julian' was in town. The crowds can be seen either side of the tank. (Black Country Society)

Harold Mills, a brilliant Walsall violinist, had taken part in Tank Week and played to crowds outside the Council House. In June 1918 he was an able seaman on board the armed merchant vessel HMS *Patia* when it was torpedoed in the Bristol Channel and sunk; thankfully he was rescued. Before the war Mills was conductor of the orchestra at Birmingham Repertory Theatre.

Women police arrive in Walsall

In January at Walsall two women police officers were appointed. This was sanctioned by the Town Council and was set to last for the duration of the war. Walsall was not the first place in the country to appoint women but was the first in the Black Country. Other areas where women were working as officers reported that their services had been of great value. Recruits were selected from women who had already been trained elsewhere, such as in London, and they would work on the same terms as male colleagues. One councillor forecast that women would continue working in the police after the war ended. However, he was against the proposal, saying he was against them 'having fancy jobs and walking about the streets in uniform'.

In May the officers, Misses Tearle and Williams, arrived at Walsall, having undergone their training in London and gained experience working in several towns. Their rate of pay was 35 shillings per week plus 10 shillings war bonus.

A policewoman as she would have looked in 1918.

Fuel rationing

Fuel rationing, including gas, electricity and coal, commenced in October. Gas and electricity rationing began once meter readings were provided and coal once the necessary requisition form was signed by the householder. Coal-hoarders, especially in larger houses, were warned that stocks would be checked and drastic action for noncompliance with regulations would be taken. Householders could take extra gas or electric rations by reducing their coal allowance but they could not convert gas or electricity allowances into coal.

World-wide flu epidemic

In July the country was in the grip of a flu epidemic and the Black Country was badly affected. The onset of the flu was very quick but in the majority of cases only lasted a couple of days. Public service workers and others had been badly affected, with the tramways in the region suffering most disruption. School attendance suffered and some schools were closed altogether. There were early deaths, mainly of young children, and doctors were under great pressure due to the demand on their services. The 1918 pandemic lasted from January 1918 until December 1920; it was unusually deadly and involved the H1N1 virus. Some 500 million people around the world were affected and between 50 and 100 million died (between 3 and 5 per cent of the world population at the time).

Early reports of the level of illness and mortality in Britain and other countries were minimized. In Britain as many as 250,000 people died from the virus. Spain, being neutral in the war, was an exception in this censorship, consequently magnifying the effects there and leading to the nickname 'Spanish Flu' being adopted. The pandemic killed mainly previously healthy young adults. This principally occurred due to a cytokine storm; an overreaction of the body's immune system.

British research identified the likely centre of the 1918 episodes as a major troop staging and hospital camp at Étaples in France. A significant virus was harboured in birds, which mutated to pigs kept near the Front.

There was also speculation that aspirin poisoning contributed to the number of fatalities. Medical advice around October 1918 was given that (relatively) high doses of the drug should be given to flu sufferers. At this time the symptoms of aspirin poisoning were not known. Furthermore, Bayer's patent on aspirin expired, meaning that more companies were able to produce the drug and flood the market, leading to increased supply and availability. This hypothesis was neither proven nor disproven.

In November the flu epidemic was still prevalent in the Black Country. There had been a number of fatalities and medical services had been stretched. Diagnosis in the early stages was difficult: symptoms included a heavy cold plus head, throat, back and limb pain and loss of appetite. Further complications included bronchitis and pneumonia, which could be fatal. To avoid contagion people were urged not to cough or sneeze in public without using a handkerchief. Quinine was thought to be helpful in relieving symptoms but could be a dangerous substance in itself: 'quackery and amateur doctoring may end disastrously.' In general, prevention was thought to be better than cure. Plenty of fresh air, with windows kept open as much as possible, was advocated; keeping warm was important but not by being in stuffy rooms. Moderate physical exercise was recommended to generate body heat.

There was plenty of advice on eating healthily, soup being highly recommended. Temperance was important for sufferers and alcohol was 'out of bounds' except for an occasional glass of old port or perhaps champagne 'in extremis'! There was no short cut to dealing with the epidemic. Schools were closed as a precaution to try to minimize the spread – especially relevant as young people were often worst affected – and there was a ban on schoolchildren going into picture houses in some areas.

Towards the end of November the epidemic worsened. In one week, forty-two people died in Walsall and arrangements were made to disinfect houses where people had died. In Bilston death rates were high during the epidemic: in November there was a total of 111 deaths in total in the town, while in the previous year the figure was only twenty-one. One family in Pelsall lost six out of eight members. In Wednesbury internments had to be carried out after nightfall due to the high death rate. Workhouses were particularly badly affected due to large numbers of people living in such close proximity. The following week things worsened again. Deaths increased, with fifty-eight in Walsall, and a further rise was expected for the following week. Coal supplies were also affected because of the flu, leading to shortages.

There was no let-up in December as the epidemic in the Black Country continued to worsen. Undertakers struggled to cope with demand and more grave-diggers had to be transferred in from other local authority work. An order was issued that burials must take place within four days of death. A local government board film was distributed for screening at local cinemas: *Dr Wise* illustrated various means of prevention and cure. By the week of Christmas the epidemic was finally abating and the death rate fell rapidly. Children were now allowed back into cinemas but many schools remained closed until January.

Women, the vote and the General Election

The campaign for women's suffrage had gained momentum throughout the early part of the nineteenth century as women became increasingly politically active. During the latter half of the century, campaign groups were formed in an attempt to lobby Members of Parliament and gain support. The Suffragette movement then began a campaign and by 1912 they were using militant tactics such as chaining themselves to railings, setting fire to mailbox contents, smashing windows and detonating bombs. Prime Minister Asquith had almost given women over 30 the right to vote. They either had to be married to a property-owner or own property themselves. However, he pulled out at the last minute as he thought women may vote against him in the next General Election, preventing his Liberals from getting into Parliament. This provoked further protest from the Suffragette movement.

Suffragette Emily Davison died under the king's horse at the Epsom Derby on 4 June 1913 while trying to pin a 'Vote for Women' banner on it. The National Union of Women's Suffrage Societies, which had always employed 'constitutional methods', lobbied during the war and compromises were worked out between them and the coalition government. The Representation of the People Act 1918 was duly passed, enfranchising women over the age of 30 who met the minimum property qualifications. Mothers living with their children were able to vote. They needed to have occupied a room or rooms for six months prior to 15 April 1918 and must own the furniture they were using. Claim forms to register were available from local council offices.

In November 1918 Prime Minister David Lloyd George launched his General Election campaign at the Grand Theatre in Wolverhampton. The task, he said, was 'to make Britain a fit country for heroes to live in.'

The General Election took place just before Christmas and among the voters in Wolverhampton was a 91-year-old woman. Polling was heavy in many areas, with a busy period from 6 to 8pm. In the new Stourbridge Division early polling was mainly by women and for the first time there were women polling clerks. One Stourbridge candidate was Miss Mary Macarthur of the Cradley women chainmakers strike fame. She had to stand in her married name, Mrs Anderson, and stood for Labour. It was felt that Labour may have won the day. One of Mary's opponents said she was a great fighter, knew what she wanted and meant to get it: 'Her methods were not exactly the ones he would have expected and it seemed to him that she made a great deal of small points.' Macarthur, however, was not returned. Some thought this was because she could not use her maiden name and lost votes because people did not associate Mary Anderson with the good work Macarthur had done. Mary was beaten by Victor Fisher, founder of the National Socialist Defence Committee, founded in 1915.

Election poster for Mary R. Macarthur. (Mrs W.C. Anderson)

The election process was a complex one, with many men still serving overseas or only recently arrived back in England. Some soldiers did not receive ballot papers allowing them to vote in the General Election, contrary to assurances that they would. Notices appeared stating that an ordinary letter or card could be used with details of the voters thereon up to 28 December. Lloyd George's coalition swept the field but results in the Black Country did not follow the rest of the nation. The Labour vote was 40 per cent, a share not reached again until the 1945 election. In Smethwick a trade unionist, J.E. Davison, defeated Suffragette leader Christabel Pankhurst. In Kingswinford the chainmakers' leader Charles Sitch comfortably won the seat for Labour. The Labour Party also won in Wednesbury and West Bromwich.

Demobilization

A week before the Armistice, Chambers of Commerce were told by the Ministry of Labour (Demobilization Department) that a number of officers would be released from the forces ahead of general demobilization. These 'pivotal men' would be those employing others. Application needed to be made setting out details of their business. Makers of bricks, cement, china clay, iron and steel were included. Miners, canal operators and the railways were among trades to which this applied. Retail firms were specifically excluded.

Chambers of Commerce were allocated places and expected to form committees to deal with applications. Non-Chamber members were allowed to apply via their local Chamber. Before the Armistice measures were drawn up for more general demobilization: essential workers who were working away from home would be provided with rail warrants and the creation of apprenticeships for young men in the forces were two of the proposals. Developments in industries suitable for women were also discussed; some wages, such as those for domestic service, would be elevated voluntarily, or rises would be made compulsory.

The Armistice
News of the Armistice reached the Black Country as it came into force. Factory hooters were blown and church bells rung. Shops and offices closed and people came out onto the streets. Almost all public houses sold out of beer but despite this, little drunkenness was reported. The day coincided with Lye Wake and the fairground was quickly filled, crowds sang songs and popular hymns and others went to church to remember the dead and bereaved. Many factories immediately suspended work and flags, banners and bunting were brought out; miners, however, carried on working. Later there were impromptu marches with improvised bands and much singing of patriotic songs.

Dudley celebrated the Armistice for a whole week and there was a firework display in the Castle Grounds. However, the town had paid a high price in men, 600 having been killed in the war. The Black Country death rate across the region during the war seemed higher than elsewhere. The Lye and Wollescote War Memorial contained 250 names, Stourbridge 377 and Amblecote 62. The Brierley Hill memorial included 205 names.

People quickly voiced opinions that Germans should be dealt with firmly for their atrocious crimes against humanity. Remembering the war we had just won, one headline read: 'This England never did, nor never shall, lie at the proud foot of a conqueror'.

Christmas 1918

Christmas recipes, mainly for cakes, were published in local newspapers. These included a fruit cake, gingerbread, pastry and 'Armistice Creams', which incorporated ground rice, dried egg, vanilla flavouring, jam and nuts. The Ministry of Food reported that meat would still be rationed for some time but the amount of meat that could be purchased for one coupon went from 4d to 5d. Pork, poultry, game and horse flesh were freed from purchase by coupon, as well as canned, potted or preserved meat and sausage. The Citrus Fruits Order was suspended due to large increases in imports. However, a warning was issued that this could be reinstated if supply or price conditions changed.

Rationing was relaxed again in time for Christmas: geese and turkey were added to the coupon-free items, but only until 4 January. There was an increase in some other coupon values from 4d to 7d and the sugar ration for Christmas week rose from 8oz to 12oz. The situation regarding rationing and coupon usage was very confusing at this time, with newspapers often publishing apparently conflicting or duplicate reports for their readers. A quantity of dried fruit had been imported and was ready for distribution; apples and oranges were also imported for sale at controlled prices. However, milk was in short supply throughout the winter and advice was given about reserving it for children. Medical advice said that children needed a pint and a half if they were aged under 18 months and a pint when over 18 months. Plenty of condensed milk was available for cooking purposes.

The Board of Trade removed restrictions on the hours when hot food could be cooked and served in hotels and restaurants, as well as the restriction on lighting for entertainments after 10.30pm for shop windows.

Christmas Eve shopping in Wolverhampton was busy. The weather was cold but dry; there were plenty of people about and plenty of goods for sale. Tradespeople and shopkeepers were having their best time for four years. Beatties reported 'our supply of suitable gifts is enormous now' but added that they would not be able to replenish stock before the New Year. In other areas Christmas was not so busy. Inflation between 1914 and the end of the war was 128 per cent and throughout the war people were constantly having to battle for pay increases to keep pace with rising prices.

In Dudley a greater than average number of carol singers made their house-to-house rounds. Parties were held for children of men who had fallen in the war and food parcels distributed to war widows.

There were still eighty wounded servicemen in Wolverhampton General Hospital on Christmas Day. The wards were decorated, cards hung and the nurses appeared in fancy dress. Traditional Christmas fare was served. All of this was done to help patients forget the war and look forward to recovery. Dudley Guest Hospital also held entertainment for their wounded, as did others around the region.

After the war

By the end of 1918 775,000 men and women had been demobilized: 270,000 from the armed forces, 115,000 POWs and 390,000 munitions workers. The release of 100,000 coal workers from the armed forces led to a warning not to expect much change in coal supplies in the short term. It was thought that many men would not want to return from the field of battle straight to the bottom of a mine and some sort of break would be needed for them. The return to work for many men was in mid-January, which meant that fuel rationing was still necessary.

Demobbed soldiers arrived home to a place that seemed not to need them. Women had taken on traditionally male roles when men went to war, such as clerks and typists, conductors and drivers on trams and factory workers. Out-of-work numbers increased weekly by 17 per 10,000 head of population.

Christmas across the Black Country had been celebrated in a relatively quiet manner; people were just happy to have their loved ones back home again. Money was now not plentiful. For example, poultry dealers struggled to sell birds at 2s 8d per pound: 'a high price to pay.'

A police officer's lot during the war had been difficult. Pay and conditions deteriorated as the war progressed and many officers were refused leave to retire or resign to obtain better-paid work. This situation boiled over in August 1918 when there were police strikes in some forces. An illegal police union was formed, which was joined by a number of officers; every officer found to have joined was dismissed. The government was taken by surprise but Lloyd George negotiated the men's return to work. There were then further strikes in 1919, which led to the setting-up of a committee chaired by Lord Desborough to

Stourbridge War Memorial in Mary Stevens Park.

deal with issues concerning pay and conditions. This led to the founding of the Police Federation, a representative body for police officers, who were forbidden to strike as part of the Desborough agreement. This organization has now been in existence for over ninety years.

By 1919 Britain and the rest of the world began to recover from more than four years of war. There was education reform, with the school leaving age being raised to 14. Housing received a boost and subsidized house-building for local authorities led to 170,000 new homes being constructed nationally. Historian A.J.P. Taylor stated that this established housing as a social service. By 1920 there was assistance for unemployed blind people and efforts were made to find employment for returning soldiers. Limiting the working week was also on the government's agenda: forty-seven or forty-eight hours was seen as the maximum per worker. A number of orders affecting trade, especially in certain metals, were suspended; a sign that the process of returning to normality had started.

Women's work during the war was lauded: 815,000 nationally worked in munitions, with 70 per cent of that work being undertaken by women. More than 5,000 served near the front lines and in total 6 million women did some work because of the war; they were largely responsible for 2 million extra acres of farmland being cultivated. The role of women in society changed forever, the work started by the Suffragette movement before the war having begun the process. By the end of the conflict, some women were eligible to vote and become candidates for election. They had worked in greater numbers in industry than ever before: from 24 per cent in 1914 to 37 per cent by the end of the war and in a wider range of occupations. This also brought forward the demise of domestic service as the principal employment for women. It was finally realized

David Lloyd George, Prime Minister from December 1916.

that women were not as weak as they were formerly supposed to have been.

A campaign began to extract money from our former enemies to compensate for excessive taxation and other costs during the war. This applied to Great Britain, the Dominions and our allies. At the Paris Peace Conference Prime Minister Lloyd George urged moderation when dealing with Germany but his was a lone voice around the table. Germany was forced to accept responsibility for the war and ordered to pay massive reparations. Lloyd George believed that the final treaty was too severe and predicted that we would be faced with war against Germany again in twenty years. How right he was!

Unlike during the Second World War, Britain did not suffer unduly financially. The main effect on Britain had been the psychological effect on the people, according to historian Correlli Barnett. However, the Great War did start to affect the British Empire, with colonies becoming more assertive as a result of their participation in the conflict.

Index